Biogenics means "life

Work out your salvation with diligence.
A philosophy comprehensive enough
to embrace the whole of knowledge
is indispensable.
A system of meditation
which will produce the power
of concentrating the mind
on anything whatsoever
is indispensable.
An art of living
which will enable us to utilize all our actions
as the best aids on the Path
is indispensable.
Be alert and strive incessantly.

—Buddha

Life always begins again.
The Angel of Earth embraces the seed
And gives unto it Life.
The kiss of the Angel of Water
Awakens the seed.
The warmth of the Angel of Sun
Makes the seed grow.
The little plant bends in the breeze—
The Angel of Air makes it grow strong.
The little plant is holy.
It bathes in the Lifestream
Of Eternal Order.

—Thanksgiving Psalms of the Dead Sea Scrolls

THE ESSENE WAY
BIOGENIC LIVING

NEW PERSPECTIVES — NEW HORIZONS — NEW FRONTIERS

by
EDMOND BORDEAUX SZEKELY

Gray are all the theories,
but green is the tree of life.
—Goethe

MCMLXXXIX
INTERNATIONAL BIOGENIC SOCIETY

SOME BOOKS BY EDMOND BORDEAUX SZEKELY

THE ESSENE WAY—BIOGENIC LIVING
THE ESSENE GOSPEL OF PEACE, BOOK ONE
BOOK TWO, THE UNKNOWN BOOKS OF THE ESSENES
BOOK THREE, LOST SCROLLS OF THE ESSENE BROTHERHOOD
BOOK FOUR, THE TEACHINGS OF THE ELECT
THE DISCOVERY OF THE ESSENE GOSPEL: The Essenes & the Vatican
SEARCH FOR THE AGELESS, in Three Volumes
THE ESSENE BOOK OF CREATION
THE ESSENE JESUS
THE ESSENE BOOK OF ASHA
THE ZEND AVESTA OF ZARATHUSTRA
ARCHEOSOPHY, A NEW SCIENCE
THE ESSENE ORIGINS OF CHRISTIANITY
TEACHINGS OF THE ESSENES FROM ENOCH TO THE DEAD SEA SCROLLS
THE ESSENES, BY JOSEPHUS AND HIS CONTEMPORARIES
THE ESSENE SCIENCE OF LIFE
THE ESSENE CODE OF LIFE
THE ESSENE SCIENCE OF FASTING AND THE ART OF SOBRIETY
ESSENE COMMUNIONS WITH THE INFINITE
THE FIRST ESSENE: The 1979 International Essene-Biogenic Seminar
THE BIOGENIC REVOLUTION: The 1977 International Essene-Biogenic Seminar
THE COSMOTHERAPY OF THE ESSENES
THE LIVING BUDDHA
THE ORIGIN OF LIFE
FATHER, GIVE US ANOTHER CHANCE
THE ECOLOGICAL HEALTH GARDEN, THE BOOK OF SURVIVAL
THE TENDER TOUCH: BIOGENIC FULFILLMENT
MAN IN THE COSMIC OCEAN
THE DIALECTICAL METHOD OF THINKING
THE EVOLUTION OF HUMAN THOUGHT
THE GREATNESS IN THE SMALLNESS
THE SOUL OF ANCIENT MEXICO
THE NEW FIRE
DEATH OF THE NEW WORLD
ANCIENT AMERICA: PARADISE LOST
PILGRIM OF THE HIMALAYAS
MESSENGERS FROM ANCIENT CIVILIZATIONS
SEXUAL HARMONY: THE NEW EUGENICS
LUDWIG VAN BEETHOVEN, PROMETHEUS OF THE MODERN WORLD
BOOKS, OUR ETERNAL COMPANIONS
THE FIERY CHARIOTS
CREATIVE WORK: KARMA YOGA
THE ART OF STUDY: THE SORBONNE METHOD
COSMOS, MAN AND SOCIETY
I CAME BACK TOMORROW
THE BOOK OF LIVING FOODS
CREATIVE EXERCISES FOR HEALTH AND BEAUTY
SCIENTIFIC VEGETARIANISM
THE CONQUEST OF DEATH
HEALING WATERS
THE BOOK OF HERBS, VITAMINS, MINERALS

Book Design by Golondrina Graphics

THE ESSENE WAY–BIOGENIC LIVING

Contents

PREFACE   *8*
  THE SPIRITUAL LEGACY OF ROMAIN ROLLAND
  THE INTERNATIONAL BIOGENIC SOCIETY

THE ESSENE WAY   *16*
  THE VISION OF ENOCH
  THE TREES OF THE EARTHLY MOTHER
  THE STARS OF THE HEAVENLY FATHER
  THE SEVENFOLD VOW
  THE BROTHERHOOD AND THE ANGELS
  FROM THE DEAD SEA SCROLLS

THE ESSENES AND THEIR TEACHING   *29*

THE ONE LAW   *32*

THE ESSENE TREE OF LIFE   *37*

THE ESSENE COMMUNIONS   *41*
  THEIR PURPOSE AND MEANING
  THE MORNING COMMUNIONS
  THE EVENING COMMUNIONS

THE NOON CONTEMPLATIONS   *50*

THE GREAT SABBATH   *51*

THE SEVENFOLD PEACE   *52*
  PEACE WITH THE BODY
  PEACE WITH THE MIND
  PEACE WITH THE FAMILY
  PEACE WITH HUMANITY
  PEACE WITH CULTURE
  PEACE WITH THE KINGDOM OF THE EARTHLY MOTHER
  PEACE WITH THE KINGDOM OF THE HEAVENLY FATHER

EXCERPTS FROM THE ESSENE GOSPEL OF PEACE   *69*

BIOGENIC LIVING   *83*

CREDO OF THE INTERNATIONAL BIOGENIC SOCIETY   *84*

WHY BIOGENIC LIVING?   *85*

BIOGENIC LIVING IN WORLD PERSPECTIVES   *87*
  VITAL SOLUTIONS TO VITAL NEEDS
  DISARMAMENT AND WORLD PEACE
  THE DESTRUCTION OF THE ENVIRONMENT
  THE SPECTRE OF WORLD STARVATION
  THE POPULATION EXPLOSION
  HABITAT AND THE BIOGENIC DWELLING
  THE BIOGENIC LIBERATION OF WOMEN
  UNEMPLOYMENT AND BREAKDOWN OF WORLD ECONOMIES
  PURE WATER: IS IT DISAPPEARING FROM OUR PLANET?
  WORLDWIDE GROWTH OF DESERTS—LESS AND LESS FERTILE LAND
  ENERGY: A LOOMING WORLDWIDE BANKRUPTCY
  SOLUTIONS THROUGH THE ESSENE WAY OF BIOGENIC LIVING

BIOGENIC NUTRITION AND BIOGENIC GARDENING *94*
    BIOGENIC NUTRITION AND THE ESSENE SCIENCE OF LIFE
    NEW SCIENTIFIC TERMINOLOGY BASED ON BIOGENIC ACTION
    THE TEN BASIC ESSENTIALS OF A PERFECT DIET
    SIMPLE, BASIC NATURAL FOODS AND THEIR SEVEN ADVANTAGES
    CELLS, ENVIRONMENTAL FLUIDS, DEFICIENCIES, DISEASE, AGING
    OUR SELF-REGENERATING POWER
    PRACTICAL ADVANTAGES OF GERMINATING AND SPROUTING
    ADVANTAGES OF SPROUTS COMPARED TO USUAL GARDENING
    EXPERIMENTAL RESEARCH FINDINGS FROM SEVEN UNIVERSITIES
    STEP-BY-STEP PRACTICAL METHOD TO GERMINATE AND SPROUT
    A CORNUCOPIA OF BIOACTIVE FOODS OF OPULENT MOTHER EARTH
    TEN IMPORTANT BIOACTIVE FRUITS OF THE ANCIENT ESSENES
    THE POTENTIALLY BIOGENIC FOODS
    BIOACTIVE BABY GREENS: INSTANT INDOOR VEGETABLE GARDEN
    A MINIATURE INDOOR HERB GARDEN
    EDUCATIONAL HEALTH AND PSYCHOLOGICAL VALUES OF INDOOR
        GARDENING FOR YOUNG AND OLD
    BIOCIDIC FOODS: HOW TO SURVIVE OUR CHEMICALIZED FOODS
        AND ENVIRONMENT
    HEALTHY DRESSINGS FOR VEGETABLE AND FRUIT SALADS
BIOGENIC LIVING *120*
    THE MIRACLE OF GRASS
    SURROUND YOURSELF WITH A LIFE-GENERATING BIOGENIC FIELD
    HOW TO MAKE A PORTABLE MEADOW
    HOW TO MAKE A BIOGENIC BATTERY
    CONTINUOUS PLANTING OF THE BIOGENIC BATTERY
    BIOGENIC RELAXATION IN THE MEADOW
    BIOGENIC SLEEP IN THE MEADOW
    BIOGENIC BREATHING IN THE MEADOW
    BIOGENIC DEW BATH
BIOGENIC DWELLING *130*
    VOLUNTARY CREATIVE SIMPLICITY
    THE BIOGENIC ECODESIC LIVING LIGHTHOUSE (BELL)
    SYMBIOSIS WITH NATURE IN THE BELL
    THE PHILOSOPHY OF THE BELL
BIOGENIC MEDITATION *140*
    ESSENE COMMUNIONS WITH THE NATURAL AND SPIRITUAL FORCES
    THE PURPOSE OF BIOGENIC MEDITATION
    HOW TO PERFORM BIOGENIC MEDITATION
    THE PRIMEVAL, ETERNAL, OMNILATERAL SUPERCOMPUTER
    HORIZONS OF THE BIOGENIC, BIODYNAMIC COMMUNIONS WITH
        OUR PRIMEVAL SELF
    MEASURABLE IMPROVEMENTS IN OUR PSYCHOPHYSIOLOGY
BIOGENIC SEXUAL FULFILLMENT *152*
    THE BIOSPHERE AND BIOGENIC ZONE OF EARTH
    HUMAN BIOGENIC ZONES—EROGENOUS ZONES—LIBIDO—ORGASM
    ANCIENT TRADITIONS FROM THE DEAD SEA SCROLLS
    DYNAMIC PRIMEVAL INTERACTION BETWEEN TERRESTRIAL AND
        HUMAN BIOGENIC FORCES
    PRESENT SEXUAL CHAOS AND THE BIOGENIC WAY OUT
    TACTILE REGENERATION AND ALTERED CONSCIOUSNESS FROM
        BIOGENIC YOUNG GRASS

THE TENDER TOUCH
BIOGENIC PSYCHOLOGY AND SELF-ANALYSIS   *161*
THE ONE LAW
THE INDIVIDUAL INVENTORY
THE SIXTEEN BIOGENIC FORCES
THE BIOGENIC EARTHLY FORCES
THE BIOGENIC COSMIC FORCES
BIOGENIC EDUCATION   *170*
THE SEVEN DEPARTMENTS OF STUDY
SEMINARS AND WORKSHOPS OF BIOGENIC LIVING
THE ALL-SIDED MICROCOSMOS OF THE BIOGENIC BATTERY   *176*
THE GREATNESS IN THE SMALLNESS
THE NATURAL FORCES IN THE BIOGENIC BATTERY
THE COSMIC FORCES IN THE BIOGENIC BATTERY
BOOK ORDER AND MEMBERSHIP APPLICATION

The Biogenic Battery

PREFACE

The year of 1928 was a memorable one in my life, as I look back from the vantage point of half a century.

To my greatest surprise, after having only mimeographed copies for three years, one of the best publishers in France, Felix Alcan, was unexpectedly willing to print my French translation of *The Essene Gospel of Peace,* the result of my intensive research in the Archives of the Vatican.* This publication, though in a modest two thousand copies, led to what was perhaps the major turning point in my life. For I suddenly had an intuition to send a copy to Romain Rolland, author of my favorite novel, *Jean Christophe.* For this magnificent epic, and for his pamphlet *Above the Battle,* a call for France and Germany to respect truth and humanity throughout their struggle in World War I, he was awarded the Nobel Prize for Literature in 1915. I did not know what to expect, but I just had to share the ideals of *The Essene Gospel of Peace* with one who had so beautifully symbolized in his story of the friendship between a young German and a young Frenchman the "harmony of opposites" which he believed could eventually be established between nations throughout the world. I dedicated his copy with these words: ". . . to the author of *The Life of Tolstoy,* and *Mahatma Gandhi*—my guide through the precarious labyrinths of the twentieth century. . ."

A week later I received an envelope, postmarked Villeneuve, Vaud. I knew immediately it was from *him.* I opened it very slowly, with the greatest care. The letter exceeded all my unspoken expectations. It was not just a formal note, thanking me for the book, but a *real* letter. One sentence particularly survived in my memory: "There is no doubt in my mind, that the common ancestral source of the basic philosophy of Tolstoy and Gandhi, without their knowing it, is the Eternal Teaching of *The Essene Gospel of Peace.*

---

*See *The Discovery of the Essene Gospel of Peace,* by Edmond Bordeaux Szekely, published by the International Biogenic Society.

It is a sublime revelation, a hymn to universal Life, to the solidarity of everything living." But the most cherished part of the letter was an invitation to visit him any afternoon of any day, "if you care to see a useless old man, retired to his garden and library, but still trying to be an active point in the universe."

A few days later I was walking along a small country road, picking here and there a few berries which grew along the path, and watching intently for the landmark of two rows of poplars which were supposed to lead to the secluded country home of M. Rolland. Finally they appeared, and I followed them to a simple rustic gate. I was received by a white-haired old lady, very dignified but friendly, who asked me to sit down in the master's library. She told me he was pruning a tree in the garden, but he would see me soon.

I was glad for a few moments to collect myself, and as I looked around the book-filled sanctuary (for it was certainly that to me), I discovered several of my old friends: a very worn copy of Epictetus, and a leatherbound copy of the *Meditations* of Marcus Aurelius, which brought back vivid memories of my school years at the Piarist monastery.* I also saw some well-used copies of books on ancient India, as well as a French translation of Tolstoy's *On Life.* Before I had the opportunity to browse among hundreds of other treasures, he suddenly appeared—dressed very simply in shirtsleeves and rumpled pants. I was immediately struck by his deep-set, burning eyes, looking at me with great warmth from a fine-boned, gaunt face, seemingly older than his sixty-odd years, marked indelibly with nobility of character, spiritual integrity, and the unmistakable genius of his art.

"So you are my young friend who translated that great masterpiece," he said, shaking my hand with surprising strength and vigor. "Sit down, and tell me about how you discovered it."

Somehow I found my tongue and tried to be as concise as I could, but I was interrupted several times by all kinds of questions which revealed his deep interest and restless mind.

*See *The Discovery of the Essene Gospel of Peace.*

9

I soon forgot my sense of awe and lost myself in a wonderful conversation which lasted about two hours (but seemed like ten minutes). Finally he sat back and fixed on me those wonderful eyes, so full of warmth, understanding, love, and what I can only describe as the wisdom of the ages. He said, "You know, you should write a book which will tell us how we can apply this ageless wisdom of the Essenes in our daily lives in this turbulent century. Give a non-religious title to it, to avoid all connotation with the orthodox churches, and try to be as practical as possible." I indicated to him my fervent accord with such an idea, but ventured some doubts as to whether or not I would be able to find a publisher for it. He smiled assuringly, and spoke these (to me) astonishing words: "If you like, I would be glad to write a preface for it, and even to put in a few good words for you with Felix Alcan." I am not often rendered speechless, but this was one of those times, and to rescue my attempts to thank him, he embraced me with these parting words: "Hard times are coming, my son. Let us unite all the forces of life against the forces of death."

The next thing I remember was walking back between the rows of poplars, scarcely believing what had happened. The world's greatest living writer had talked with me for more than two hours and had offered to write the preface to my next book! And he had actually advised me to write this book! It took me several miles of walking and many handfuls of berries before I gradually returned to a somewhat more normal state of mind.

I set to work right away, finishing the book in three months. I sent him the manuscript, wondering as I mailed it if my whole experience had not been a wonderful dream, after all. If it was, it was a shared dream, for soon I received from M. Rolland a preface which again exceeded my expectations— a beautiful essay containing his prophecy of the coming depression and world war (which explained the meaning of his cryptic parting words. "Hard times are coming,") and the possible ways of recuperation afterwards. He ended the preface with that unforgettable imperative which still rang in my ears: "Let us unite all the forces of life against the forces of death."

My book, *La Vie Biogenique* (Biogenic Living), was received with great enthusiasm, especially among the young. It became a kind of bible for the many groups of young boys and girls who at that time were gravitating to the balmy climate of the south of France, living in small cooperatives (not communes), trying to establish a new way of life which would make impossible the kind of war their parents had suffered. They were wonderful, starry-eyed idealists, carrying in one hand *The Essene Gospel of Peace,* and in the other, *La Vie Biogenique.* I remember with particular fondness a small band of French Essenes whom I helped to get organized in a practical way to live a simple, natural, creative, spiritual life, following the precepts of my two books. I wrote about them in volume one of *Search for the Ageless,** trying to memorialize them and their heroic efforts. For their dreams were short-lived. The war of their parents was destined to repeat itself on an even larger scale, and Romain Rolland's prophecy came sadly true.

I lost all contact with France when I left, just before the war, to start my ethnological and archeological research work over the five continents (described in volume one of *Search for the Ageless*), and France experienced a series of events which changed that country forever: the war, the German occupation, post war crises, etc. It was not until 1975 that something happened which brought back that whole wonderful dream-like period between the wars.

In a little book store in Costa Rica, I accidentally discovered a French edition of my *Essene Gospel of Peace,* and in its preface I learned to my great surprise that I had perished in a shipwreck in the Gulf of Mexico in 1938! (The shipwreck was real enough, but I obviously survived, thanks to Essene methods described in *Search for the Ageless.*) The writer of this sad news went on to deplore the fact that due to my untimely demise the opportunity to obtain and publish Books Two and Three of *The Essene Gospel of Peace* was lost forever. This prompted me to send a humorous

*See Volume One of *Search for the Ageless,* by Edmond Bordeaux Szekely, available from the International Biogenic Society.

letter to the publisher, Pierre Genillard of Geneva, informing him that the rumors of my death were greatly exaggerated, and that I was not only very much alive, but had already written and seen the publication of the two remaining volumes of *The Essene Gospel of Peace* in English.

In due time I received a rather shaky letter from Pierre Genillard celebrating "la resurrection de Dr. Bordeaux," and assuring me he would modify the preface of the next edition of the Essene Gospel. Apparently he did so, because two years later in California, just before the opening session of the 1977 International Essene Seminar (which I conduct every year) I received an unexpected phone call from Paris. The connection was remarkably good (it most likely came by satellite), and the first thing I heard was the clamor of many voices all trying to talk at once. Their spokesman, Pierre, finally took over and told me an amazing story.

When I left France, as I mentioned before, I also left in several small Essene cooperative communities that I had helped to establish, a brave band of young, idealistic pioneers of a new way of life—a life based on voluntary, creative simplicity inspired by the ancient Essene Brotherhood. The war and occupation not only brought the communities to an end, but dispersed the young people in a tragic way: some were killed outright by Nazis, others died fighting in the underground, still others died in concentration camps. But some did survive, and later raised families, their children growing up in a totally different world, unaware of their parents' dreams of an ideal Essene society. They completely forgot my books and joined the establishment, becoming government officials, businessmen, etc., relegating their parents' Essene literature to the attic, the basement, or the top dusty shelves of a little-used library. Still, perhaps for unknown subconscious reasons, they maintained contact with each other, and when they in turn married and had children, these children—the grandchildren of my first young Essenes—somehow began to pull out of dusty nooks and crannies, out of ancient cracked suitcases in the attic, out of forgotten cardboard boxes in a basement corner, my books. And these young boys and girls—like a reincarnation of

André, Renée, Marcel, and all the rest—wholeheartedly embraced the ageless Essene teachings and biogenic principles and decided to revive those ideals for which their grandparents had given their lives. In my book, *La Vie Biogenique,* the same book I had written with Romain Rolland's blessing, they found a practical guide to carrying out the principles embodied in the poetry of *The Essene Gospel of Peace,* and (though convinced I was dead, due to the moving obituary they read in that preface to the French edition) enthusiastically organized themselves into an impressive movement, the *Societé Biogenique Internationale.* It was only after they were well established, with a growing and thriving membership, that they read in a new French edition of the Essene Gospel (that my letter had inspired) the incredible news that I was alive and well, resurrected from my watery grave. (The preface had the title, *La Resurrection de Dr. Bordeaux.*) They tracked down my location, got my phone number, and now they were on the long-distance line, excitedly telling me that they were my "spiritual grandchildren" and were "carrying the torch" for a whole new generation of Biogenic Essenes.

Well, I was at once astonished, delighted, and deeply moved. I felt again that sense of awe at the power of the Essene teachings to move the hearts of truth-seeking idealists, no matter what their background, nationality, station in life, age, etc. The power of the truth and nothing else had inspired these young people and set them on the path of their grandparents, and before them, brave idealistic intellectuals in each preceding generation. We reluctantly hung up, after having sealed a bargain that they would send a delegation of twelve to represent the French Essene Biogenic Movement at our next 1978 International Essene Seminar.

And now it was my turn to be inspired. I decided it was the least I could do, after having been resurrected from my shipwreck, to do some resurrecting of my own. I resolved to reconstruct my 1928 book on Biogenic Living, adapting it to the present world conditions. Voilà, the origin of this book: *The Essene Way—Biogenic Living.*

Now a few words about the International Biogenic Society.

In 1928, when I received the proofs of *La Vie Biogenique* from the publisher, Felix Alcan asked me if I had any idea what to do with an extra two pages remaining at the end. I remembered the words of Romain Rolland about helping people to apply in a practical way the principles of the Essene Gospel, and I drew up the statutes of an international fraternal organization, to bring together men and women of good will everywhere, putting aside everything which might divide us and concentrating on all things which would unite us; in the words of Romain Rolland, "to unite all the forces of life against the forces of death." I sent the text for the two pages to Romain Rolland, asking him if he would like to be the President of the "International Biogenic Society," as I called it. He answered with a warm letter, saying that although he was too old to take an active part in such an organization, he would be honored to be the co-founder with me, saying that I "had the physical stamina of youth to carry the torch in the darkness." Well, it was I who was honored and elated to be considered a co-founder with Romain Rolland, and after signing both our names to the statutes, I sent the manuscript to Felix Alcan, who printed it faithfully on the last two pages of my book. These were the two pages which inspired not only my "spiritual grandchildren" to reorganize the International Biogenic Society in France, but also inspired me to reinstitute it in the United States, hoping it would flourish as successfully as it has there.

The first six months of its new existence have exceeded all my imaginings. The Essene Way of Biogenic Living, as expressed through the International Biogenic Society, has doubled, tripled, and quadrupled its number of followers, and the end is not in sight. It now has a large membership not only all over the United States but in all the English-speaking countries and in many other parts of the world. To celebrate, it gives me special satisfaction to mark this 50th year of the founding of the International Biogenic Society with the publication of *The Essene Way—Biogenic Living*— actually a re-publication and reincarnation of my original *La Vie Biogenique*—child of mine and godchild of Romain Rolland in 1928.

If this English language edition of my original publication in French will stimulate the reader to become an active point in the universe and join the membership of the International Biogenic Society, then the purpose of my book will be accomplished. I have never forgotten, nor will I ever forget, the words of Romain Rolland as we parted under the tall poplars that long-ago day in France: "Let us put aside everything that divides us, and concentrate on all the things which unite us. Let us mobilize all the forces of Life against the forces of death."

EDMOND BORDEAUX SZEKELY

Forest Home, British Columbia, 1977.

THE ESSENE WAY

O that my words
Were graven with an iron pen
In the rock forever!
For I know that my Creator liveth:
And he shall stand at the end of time
Upon the earth and the stars.
And though worms destroy this body
Yet shall I see God.

—*Thanksgiving Psalms of the Dead Sea Scrolls*

Oh, the Ancient Truth!
Ages upon ages past it was found,
And it bound together a Noble Brotherhood.
The Ancient Truth!
Hold fast to it!

—*Goethe*

THE VISION OF ENOCH

THE MOST ANCIENT REVELATION

God Speaks to Man

I speak to you.
Be still
Know
I am
God.

I spoke to you
When you were born.
I spoke to you
At your first sight.
I spoke to you
At your first word.
I spoke to you
At your first thought.
I spoke to you
At your first love.
I spoke to you
At your first song.

I speak to you
Through the grass of the meadows.
I speak to you
Through the trees of the forests.
I speak to you
Through the valleys and the hills.
I speak to you
Through the Holy Mountains.
I speak to you
Through the rain and the snow.
I speak to you
Through the waves of the sea.
I speak to you
Through the dew of morning.
I speak to you
Through the peace of evening.

I speak to you
Through the splendor of the sun.
I speak to you
Through the brilliant stars.
I speak to you
Through the storm and the clouds.
I speak to you
Through the mysterious rainbow.

I will speak to you
When you are alone.
I will speak to you
Through the Wisdom of the Ancients.
I will speak to you
At the end of time.
I will speak to you
When you have seen my Angels.
I will speak to you
Throughout Eternity.

I speak to you.
Be still
Know
I am
God.

—from *The Essene Gospel of Peace, Book Two:*
The Unknown Books of the Essenes

THE TREES OF THE EARTHLY MOTHER

Go towards the high growing Trees,
And before one of them
Which is beautiful, high growing and mighty,
Say thou these words:
Hail be unto Thee!
O good living Tree,
Made by the Creator.

In the days of old, when the Creation was young,
The earth was filled with giant trees,
Whose branches soared above the clouds,
And in them dwelled our Ancient Fathers,
They who walked with the Angels,
And who lived by the Holy Law.
In the shadow of their branches all men lived in peace,
And wisdom and knowledge was theirs,
And the revelation of the Endless Light.
Through their forests flowed the Eternal River,
And in the center stood the Tree of Life,
And it was not hidden from them.
They ate from the table of the Earthly Mother,
And slept in the arms of the Heavenly Father,
And their covenant was for eternity with the Holy Law.
In that time the trees were the brothers of men,
And their span on the earth was very long,
As long as the Eternal River,
Which flowed without ceasing
From the Unknown Spring.
Now the desert sweeps the earth with burning sand,
The giant trees are dust and ashes
And the wide river is a pool of mud.
For the sacred covenant with the Creator
Was broken by the sons of men,
And they were banished from their home of trees.
Now the path leading to the Tree of Life
Is hidden from the eyes of men,
And sorrow fills the empty sky
Where once the lofty branches soared.

Now into the burning desert
Come the Children of Light,
To labor in the Garden of the Brotherhood.
The seed they plant in the barren soil
Will become a mighty forest,
And trees shall multiply
And spread their wings of green
Until the whole earth be covered once again.
The whole earth shall be a garden,
And the tall trees shall cover the land.
In that day shall sing the Children of Light a new song:
My brother, Tree!
Let me not hide myself from thee,
But let us share the breath of life
Which our Earthly Mother hath given to us.
More beautiful than the finest jewel
Of the rugmaker's art,
Is the carpet of green leaves under my bare feet;
More majestic than the silken canopy
Of the rich merchant,
Is the tent of branches above my head,
Through which the bright stars give light.
The wind among the leaves of the cypress
Maketh a sound like unto a chorus of angels.

—from *The Essene Gospel of Peace, Book Three:*
Lost Scrolls of the Essene Brotherhood

THE STARS OF THE HEAVENLY FATHER

The white, shining,
Far seen Stars!
The piercing, health-bringing,
Far-piercing Stars!
Their shining rays,
Their brightness and glory
Are all, through thy Holy Law,
The Speakers of thy praise,
O Heavenly Father!

Over the face of heaven
Did the Heavenly Father hurl his might:
And lo! He did leave a River of Stars in his wake!
We invoke the bright and glorious Stars
That wash away all things of fear
And bring health and life unto all Creations.
We invoke the bright and glorious Stars
To which the Heavenly Father
Hath given a thousand senses,
The glorious Stars that have within themselves
The Seed of Life and of Water.
Unto the bright and glorious Stars
Do we offer up an Invocation:
With wisdom, power and love,
With speech, deeds and rightly-spoken words,
Do we sacrifice unto the bright and glorious Stars
That fly towards the Heavenly Sea
As swiftly as the arrow
Darteth through heavenly Space.
We invoke the bright and glorious Stars,
That stand out beautiful,
Spreading comfort and joy
As they commune within themselves.
We invoke the Lord of the Stars,
The Angel of Light,
The ever-awake!
Whose face looketh over

All the seven and seven Kingdoms of the Earth.
The Heavenly Order pervades all things pure,
Whose are the Stars,
In whose Light the glorious Angels are clothed.
Great is our Heavenly Father, and of great power:
His understanding is infinite.
He telleth the number of the stars:
He calleth them all by their names.
Behold the height of the stars!
How high they are!
Yet the Heavenly Father doth hold them in his palms.
Traversed by the continual Stars
Shall the souls of the Children of Light
Take wing and join the Angels of the Heavenly Father.
Then shall the Eternal Sea
Reflect the shining glory of the heavens,
And the branches of the Tree of Life reach to the Stars.
Then shall the Kingdom of Heaven
Fill all the earth with Glory,
And the shining Stars of the most High
Shall blaze within the hearts of the Children of Light
And warm and comfort the seeking sons of men.

—from *The Essene Gospel of Peace, Book Three:*
Lost Scrolls of the Essene Brotherhood

THE SEVENFOLD VOW

I want to and will do my best
To live like the Tree of Life,
Planted by the Great Masters of our Brotherhood,
With my Heavenly Father,
Who planted the Eternal Garden of the Universe
And gave me my spirit;
With my Earthly Mother
Who planted the Great Garden of the Earth
And gave me my body;
With my brothers
Who are working in the Garden of our Brotherhood.

I want to and will do my best
To hold every morning my Communions
With the Angels of the Earthly Mother,
And every evening
With the Angels of the Heavenly Father,
As established by
The Great Masters of our Brotherhood.

I want to and will do my best
To follow the path of the Sevenfold Peace.

I want to and will do my best
To perfect my body which acts,
My body which feels,
And my body which thinks,
According to the Teachings
Of the Great Masters of our Brotherhood.

I will always and everywhere obey with reverence
My Master,
Who gives me the Light
Of the Great Masters of all times.

I will submit to my Master
And accept his decision
On whatever differences or complaints I may have
Against any of my brothers
Working in the Garden of the Brotherhood.

I will always and everywhere keep secret
All the traditions of our Brotherhood
Which my Master will tell me;
And I will never reveal to anyone these secrets
Without the permission of my Master;
And I will always give credit to him
For all this knowledge.
I will never use the knowledge and power I have gained
Through initiation from my Master
For material or selfish purposes.

I enter the Eternal and Infinite Garden
With reverence to the Heavenly Father,
To the Earthly Mother, and
To the Great Masters,
Reverence to the Holy,
Pure and Saving Teaching,
Reverence to the Brotherhood of the Elect.

—from *The Essene Gospel of Peace, Book Three:*
Lost Scrolls of the Essene Brotherhood

THE BROTHERHOOD AND THE ANGELS

PROLOGUE

When God saw that his people would perish
Because they did not see the Light of life,
He chose the best of Israel,
So that they might make the Light of Life
To shine before the sons of men.
And those chosen were called Essenes,
Because they taught the ignorant
And healed the sick,
And they gathered on the evening of every seventh day
To rejoice with the Angels.

WORSHIP

ELDER: Earthly Mother, Give us the Food of Life!

BROTHERS: We will eat the Food of Life!

ELDER: Angel of Sun, give us the Fire of Life!

BROTHERS: We will perpetuate the Fire of Life!

ELDER: Angel of Water, give us the Water of Life!

BROTHERS: We will bathe in the Water of Life!

ELDER: Angel of Air, give us the Breath of Life!

BROTHERS: We will breathe the Air of Life!

ELDER: Heavenly Father, give us thy Power!

BROTHERS: We will build the Kingdom of God with the Power of the Heavenly Father!

ELDER: Heavenly Father, give us thy Love!

BROTHERS: We will fill our hearts with the Love of the Heavenly Father!

ELDER: Heavenly Father, give us thy Wisdom!

BROTHERS: We will follow the Wisdom of the Heavenly Father!

ELDER: Heavenly Father, give us Eternal Life!

BROTHERS: We will live like the Tree of Eternal Life!

ELDER: Peace be with thee!

BROTHERS: Peace be with thee!

—from *The Essene Gospel of Peace, Book Three:*
Lost Scrolls of the Essene Brotherhood

FROM THE DEAD SEA SCROLLS

I thank Thee, Heavenly Father,
because Thou hast put me
at a source of running streams,
at a living spring in a land of drought,
watering an eternal garden of wonders,
the Tree of Life, mystery of mysteries,
growing everlasting branches for eternal planting
to sink their roots into the stream of life
from an eternal source.
And Thou, Heavenly Father,
protect their fruits
with the angels of the day
and of the night
and with flames of Eternal Light burning every way.

from the Thanksgiving Psalms
of the Dead Sea Scrolls

I will praise Thy works
with songs of Thanksgiving
continually, from period to period,
in the circuits of the day, and in its fixed order;
with the coming of light from its source
and at the turn of evening and the outgoing of light,
at the outgoing of darkness and the coming in of day,
continually,
in all the generations of time.

from the Thanksgiving Psalms
of the Dead Sea Scrolls

For Further Reading:
The Essene Gospel of Peace, Books I, II, III and IV
Teachings of the Essenes, from Enoch to the Dead Sea Scrolls
The Essene Book of Asha

THE ESSENES AND THEIR TEACHING

From the remote ages of antiquity a remarkable teaching has existed which is universal in its application and ageless in its wisdom. Fragments of it are found in Sumerian hieroglyphs and on tiles and stones dating back some eight or ten thousand years. Some of the symbols, such as for the sun, moon, air, water and other natural forces, are from an even earlier age preceding the cataclysm that ended the Pleistocene period. How many thousands of years previous to that the teaching existed is unknown.

To study and practice this teaching is to reawaken within every heart an intuitive knowledge that can solve one's individual problems and the problems of the world.

Traces of the teaching have appeared in almost every country and religion. Its fundamental principles were taught in ancient Persia, Egypt, India, Tibet, China, Palestine, Greece and many other countries. It was transmitted in one of its purest and most unique forms by the Essenes, that mysterious brotherhood which lived during the last two or three centuries B.C. and the first century of the Christian era at the Dead Sea in Palestine and at Lake Mareotis in Egypt. In Palestine and Syria the members of the brotherhood were known as Essenes, and in Egypt as Therapeutae, or healers.

The teaching appears in the Zend Avesta of Zarathustra, who translated it into a way of life that was followed for thousands of years. It contains the fundamental concepts of Brahmanism, the Vedas, and the Upanishads; and the Yoga systems of India sprang from the same source. Buddha later gave forth essentially the same basic ideas, and his sacred Bodhi tree is correlated with the Essene Tree of Life. In Tibet the teaching once more found expression in the Tibetan Wheel of Life.

The Pythagoreans and Stoics in ancient Greece also followed the Essene principles and much of their way of life. The same teaching was an element of the Adonic culture of the Phoenicians, of the Alexandrian School of Philosophy in Egypt, and contributed greatly to many branches of

Western culture, Freemasonry, Gnosticism, the Kabala and Christianity. Jesus interpreted it in its most sublime and beautiful form in the seven Beatitudes of the Sermon on the Mount.

The Essenes lived on the shores of lakes and rivers, away from cities and towns, and practiced a communal way of life, sharing equally in everything. They were mainly agriculturists and arboriculturists, having a vast knowledge of crops, soil and climatic conditions which enabled them to grow a great variety of fruits and vegetables in comparatively desert areas and with a minimum of labor.

They had no servants or slaves and were said to have been the first people to condemn slavery both in theory and practice. There were no rich and no poor amongst them, both conditions being considered by them as deviations from the Law. They established their own economic system, based wholly on the Law, and showed that all man's food and material needs can be attained without struggle, through knowledge of the Law.

They spent much time in study both of ancient writings and special branches of learning, such as education, healing and astronomy. They were said to be the heirs of Chaldean and Persian astronomy and Egyptian arts of healing. They were adept in prophecy for which they prepared by prolonged fasting. In the use of plants and herbs for healing man and beast they were likewise proficient.

They lived a simple regular life, rising each day before sunrise to study and commune with the forces of nature, bathing in cold water as a ritual and donning white garments. After their daily labor in the fields and vineyards they partook of their meals in silence, preceding and ending them with prayer. They were entirely vegetarian in their eating and never touched flesh foods nor fermented liquids. Their evenings were devoted to study and communion with the heavenly forces.

Their way of life enabled them to live to advanced ages of 120 years or more and they were said to have marvelous strength and endurance. In all their activities they expressed creative love.

They sent out healers and teachers from the brotherhoods, amongst whom were Elijah, John the Baptist, John the Beloved and the great Essene Master, Jesus.

Records of the Essene way of life have come down to us from writings of their contemporaries. Pliny, the Roman naturalist, Philo the Alexandrian philosopher, Josephus the Roman-Jewish historian, Solanius and others spoke of them variously as "a race by themselves, more remarkable than any other in the world," "the oldest of the initiates, receiving their teaching from Central Asia," "teaching perpetuated through an immense space of ages," "constant and unalterable holiness."

Some of the outer teaching is preserved in Aramaic text in the Vatican in Rome. Some in Slavic text was found in the possession of the Habsburgs in Austria and said to have been brought out of Asia in the thirteenth century by Nestorian priests fleeing the hordes of Genghis Khan.

Echoes of the teaching exist today in many forms, in rituals of the Masons, in the seven-branched candlestick, in the greeting "Peace be with you," used from the time of Moses.

From its antiquity, its persistence through the ages, it is evident the teaching could not have been the concept of any individual or any people, but is the interpretation, by a succession of great Teachers, of the Law of the universe, the basic Law, eternal and unchanging as the stars in their courses, the same now as two or ten thousand years ago, and as applicable today as then.

For Further Reading:
The Discovery of the Essene Gospel of Peace
The Essene Book of Creation
The Essenes, by Josephus
The Essene Origins of Christianity
The Fiery Chariots
Search for the Ageless, Volume One
Essene Communions with the Infinite

THE ONE LAW

The teachings which Moses brought forth at Mount Sinai were practiced fifteen hundred years later by the Essene Brotherhoods in Palestine and Egypt.

To understand his teachings is to understand the values the Essene practices have for man today.

Moses was the giver of the Law, the One Law. He established the monotheism that was to become not only the fundamental tenet of the Essene Brotherhoods but of all western civilization. The most authoritative information we have about his teaching comes from their Brotherhoods.

Their tradition divides his life into three periods symbolic of the experiences in every man's life. In the first period of forty years, during which he lived as a prince of Egypt, he followed the path of tradition, acquiring all the education and knowledge available.

In the second period of his life he spent forty years in the desert following the path of nature, studying the book of nature, as have many other great geniuses and prophets, including Jesus. In the huge vastnesses of the desert, with their solitude and silence, great inner truths have been brought forth. In this period of his life, Moses discovered the One Law, the totality of all laws. He found that this one Law governed all manifestations of life, and it governed the whole universe. To him it was the greatest of all miracles to find that everything operates under one law. Then he came upon the idea of the totality of laws. And this totality he called the Law, spelled with a capital "L."

He first observed that man lives in a dynamic, constantly changing universe; plants and animals grow and disappear; moons wax and wane. There is no static point in nature or man. He saw that the Law manifests in perpetual change, and that behind the change is a plan of Cosmic Order on a vast scale.

He came to understand that the Law is the greatest and only power in the universe and that all other laws and all things are a part of the one Law. The Law is subject to no other law or laws. It is eternal, indestructible, incapable of defeat. A plant, a tree, a human body or a solar system each has its own laws, mathematical, biological and astronomical. But the one supreme power, the Law, is behind all of them.

The Law governs all that takes place in the universe, and all other universes, all activity, all creation, mental or physical. It governs all that exists in physical manifestation, in energy and power, in consciousness, all knowledge, all thought, all feeling, all reality. The Law creates life and it creates thought.

The sum total of life on all the planets in the universe was called by the Essenes the cosmic ocean of life. And the sum total of currents of thought in the universe was called the cosmic ocean of thought, or cosmic consciousness in more modern terminology.

This cosmic ocean of life and cosmic ocean of thought form a dynamic unity of which man is an inseparable part. Every thinking body of every individual is in constant inner communion with this unity. Every human being is an individualized part of the unity. This unity is the Law, the Eternal Light, of which Moses spoke.

The third period of Moses' life, the Exodus, began when he determined to dedicate the remainder of his days to the realization and application of the Law, and to bringing mankind into harmony with it. He recognized the enormity of the task before him in attempting to make both the ignorant masses and the arrogant rulers accept the Law and live in harmony with it. Seemingly insurmountable obstacles confront all world reformers, when pure idea meets the opposing force in the inertia of the human mind and the resistance of entrenched power. It represents a revolution of the dynamic against the static, of higher values against pseudo-values, of freedom against slavery, and it is not limited to one time in history, nor to mankind as a whole, but occurs repeatedly in the life of individual man.

When Moses found he could not change the Egyptian rulers or the masses of the people, he turned to the small minority, the enslaved and oppressed people of Israel, hoping to convert them and establish a new nation based wholly on the Law. He is the only figure in universal history that did establish such a nation.

Moses saw the universe as a gigantic Cosmic Order in which existed inexhaustible sources of energy, knowledge and harmony at man's disposal. He had always remembered the two legends of his ancestor Jacob who had fought and conquered an angel and later had had a vision of angels ascending and descending upon a ladder connecting heaven and earth. He identified these angels as the forces of nature and the powers of man's consciousness and saw that these forces and powers were the connecting link between man and God. He identified God with the great universal Law.

He came to the conclusion that if man is to reach God, he must first become master of all the forces which are manifestations of God, of the Law. This was the foundation of occult science as it is termed today, of the science of the angels, later recorded as angelology.

Moses wanted his followers to realize that they are in constant contact, every moment of their lives and in all points of their being, with all the forces of life and the visible and invisible universe; and if they contact these powers consciously, and become continually conscious of them, they will enjoy perfect health, happiness and harmony in body and mind and in every department of their lives.

In later Essene traditions the abstract idea of the Law was conveyed by the symbol of a tree, called the Tree of Life. Moses had received a great revelation when he saw the burning bush in the desert. This represented two aspects of universal life: warmth and light. The warmth of the fire symbolized the fire of life, vitality in the material world. The light, symbolizing man's consciousness, represented the light of wisdom as opposed to the darkness of ignorance in the immaterial universe. Together they represent the whole universe and the idea that man in the center draws life and vitality from all the forces of the cosmos.

The Essenes symbolized this teaching in their Tree of Life which pictured to them in a concrete form that man was a unity of energy, thoughts and emotions and a unit of life force constantly communing with the totality of energies in the universe. Moses wished to see man living in harmony with the laws which govern all these energies inside and outside man, and to become conscious of them and utilize them in every moment of life.

In his study of the totality of the Law Moses attained an intuitive knowledge of the origin of the world and the beginning of all things. It was from this beginning of all things that he derived the laws for daily life. He learned that all things are parts of the whole, put together according to law; and the seven elements or basic forces of life appeared in seven great cycles of creation, one element in each cycle. He grouped the days of the week into a corresponding cycle of seven, considering each day to correspond to a different one of the elements. This was symbolized in Essene traditions by the seven-branched candlestick, the candles of which were lit every seventh day, the sabbath, to remind man of the seven cycles and the seven basic forces of the visible world and the seven basic powers of the invisible world of man's consciousness.

The three periods of Moses' life, in which he discovered the Law and its manifestations, represent the three periods into which nearly every man's life can be divided. The first, Egypt, has been called the period of bondage, of the darkness of ignorance, when the free flow of vital energy is obstructed by ignorance and false values. Mankind's Egypt, his slavery, consists in the totality of his deviations from the Law.

The second period in Moses' life corresponds to the desert in an individual's life when his false values fall away and he sees nothing but emptiness ahead of him. It is in this period man most urgently needs inner guidance that he may find his way back to the Light, the Law.

The third period, the Exodus, is possible for every man. There is always the Light showing the way to the exodus. Man's Egypt of bondage is never eternal. The Exodus under Moses lasted forty years, but it was only a beginning on the path of intuition, the path of learning to live in harmony with the laws of life, of nature and the cosmos. An exodus for humanity can only be accomplished through the cumulative efforts of many people over many generations.

But it can be accomplished and it will be accomplished. There is always a Canaan, which is not a mythical utopia, but a living reality. The exodus is the path that leads toward Canaan, the path that Moses trod, the path to which the Essene practices light the way.

For Further Reading:
The Essene Book of Creation
Teachings of the Essenes from Enoch to the Dead Sea Scrolls
The Essene Jesus
The Essene Book of Asha
The Essene Code of Life
The Essene Teachings of Zarathustra

THE ESSENE TREE OF LIFE

Man has appeared to realize, as far back as records exist, that he was surrounded by invisible forces. In culture after culture of the past he has used a certain symbolism to express his relationship to these forces in the midst of which he moves. This mystical symbol which has been imbedded in almost all religions and occult teachings is called the Tree of Life. In outer legend and inner wisdom man's deepest intuitions have focussed about it.

It was considered by Zarathustra as the law itself and was the center of his philosophy and way of thinking. In the hidden teachings of Moses, the Essene Book of Genesis, it was the Tree of Knowledge in the Garden of Eden guarded by angels. The Essenes called it the Tree of Life.

To the earlier concepts of the Tree the Essenes added what the ancient writers called Angelology. This Science of the Angels was brought forth by the Essenes at their brotherhood at the Dead Sea. Their angels were the forces in the universe.

It was known by many of the ancient peoples that these invisible forces were a source of energy and power, and that man's life was sustained by contact with them. They knew that to the degree he was able to utilize these forces, he would move forward in his individual evolution in body and spirit, and as he put himself in harmony with them, his life would prosper. Certain of the people not only knew of these forces but had specific methods of contacting and utilizing them.

The Essene Tree of Life represented fourteen positive forces, seven of them heavenly or cosmic forces and seven earthly or terrestrial forces. The Tree was pictured as having seven roots reaching down into the earth and seven branches extending up toward the heavens, thus symbolizing man's relationship to both earth and heaven. Man was pictured in the center of the tree halfway between heaven and earth.

The use of the number seven is an integral part of the Essene tradition which has been transmitted to Western cultures in various outer ways, such as the seven days of the week.

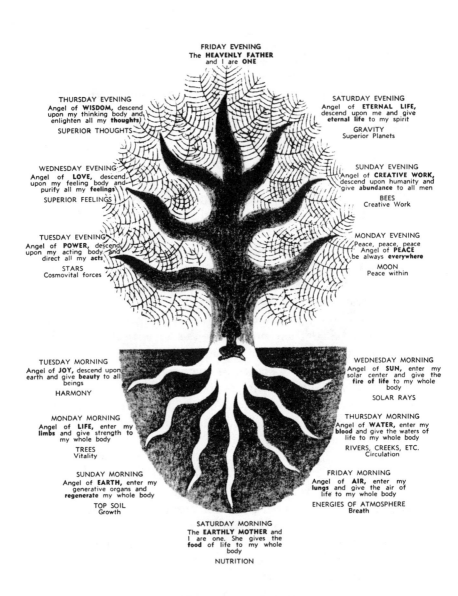

FRIDAY EVENING
The **HEAVENLY FATHER**
and I are ONE

THURSDAY EVENING
Angel of **WISDOM**, descend
upon my thinking body and
enlighten all my **thoughts**
SUPERIOR THOUGHTS

SATURDAY EVENING
Angel of **ETERNAL LIFE,**
descend upon me and give
eternal life to my spirit
GRAVITY
Superior Planets

WEDNESDAY EVENING
Angel of **LOVE**, descend
upon my feeling body and
purify all my **feelings**
SUPERIOR FEELINGS

SUNDAY EVENING
Angel of **CREATIVE WORK,**
descend upon humanity and
give **abundance** to all men
BEES
Creative Work

TUESDAY EVENING
Angel of **POWER**, descend
upon my acting body and
direct all my **acts**
STARS
Cosmovital forces

MONDAY EVENING
Peace, peace, peace
Angel of **PEACE**
be always **everywhere**
MOON
Peace within

TUESDAY MORNING
Angel of **JOY**, descend upon
earth and give **beauty** to all
beings
HARMONY

WEDNESDAY MORNING
Angel of **SUN**, enter my
solar center and give the
fire of life to my whole
body
SOLAR RAYS

MONDAY MORNING
Angel of **LIFE**, enter my
limbs and give strength to
my whole body
TREES
Vitality

THURSDAY MORNING
Angel of **WATER**, enter my
blood and give the waters of
life to my whole body
RIVERS, CREEKS, ETC.
Circulation

SUNDAY MORNING
Angel of **EARTH**, enter my
generative organs and
regenerate my whole body
TOP SOIL
Growth

FRIDAY MORNING
Angel of **AIR**, enter my
lungs and give the air of
life to my whole body
ENERGIES OF ATMOSPHERE
Breath

SATURDAY MORNING
The **EARTHLY MOTHER** and
I are one. She gives the
food of life to my whole
body
NUTRITION

THE ESSENE TREE OF LIFE
with the Morning and Evening Communions

Each root and branch of the tree represented a different force or power. The roots represented the forces of earth: the Earthly Mother, the Angel of Earth, the Angel of Life, the Angel of Joy, the Angel of Sun, the Angel of Water and the Angel of Air. The seven branches represented cosmic powers: the Heavenly Father, and his Angels of Eternal Life, Creative Work, Peace, Power, Love and Wisdom. These were the Essene angels of the visible and invisible worlds.

In ancient Hebrew and Medieval literature these heavenly and earthly forces or angels were given names, Michael, Gabriel, and so on; and they were pictured in religious art as human figures with wings and clad in flowing robes, such as in the frescoes of Michelangelo.

Man, in the center of the Tree, was seen to be surrounded as in a magnetic field, by all the forces, or angels, of heaven and earth. He was pictured as in the meditation posture, the upper half of his body above the ground and the lower half in the earth. This indicated that part of man is allied to the forces of heaven and part to the forces of earth.

This position of man in the center of the Tree, with the earthly forces below him and the heavenly forces above, also corresponds to the position of the organs in the physical body. The gastric and generative tracts in the lower half of the body, being instruments of self-preservation and self-perpetuation, belong to the earthly forces. Whereas the lungs and brain, in the upper half of the body, are the instruments of breathing and thinking and thus connect man with the finer forces of the universe.

Contact with the angelic forces represented by the Tree of Life was the very essence of the daily life of the Essenes. They knew that to be in harmony with these forces they must make conscious effort to contact them. The Essenes were spoken of by the ancient writers as an extremely practical people. Their concepts were not just theories; they knew exactly how to be continually aware of the forces about them and how to absorb their power and put them into action in their daily lives.

They had the deep wisdom to understand that these forces were sources of energy, knowledge and harmony by which man can transform his organism into a more and more sensitive instrument to receive and consciously utilize the forces. Furthermore, they considered that to put himself into harmony with the forces of the Heavenly Father and the Earthly Mother was man's most important activity in life.

The characteristics of each one of the different forces was very clear to them and they knew what the force meant in each individual's life and how it should be utilized.

They also understood the relationship between the forces. They considered that each heavenly force has an earthly force corresponding to it and each earthly force a corresponding heavenly power. These corresponding heavenly and earthly forces were placed on the Essene Tree of Life diagonally across from each other, one above and one below man. A line drawn between any two corresponding forces consequently passed directly through man in the center of the Tree.

The forces which correspond with each other, above and below, are as follows:

THE HEAVENLY FATHER AND THE EARTHLY MOTHER
THE ANGEL OF ETERNAL LIFE AND THE ANGEL OF EARTH
THE ANGEL OF CREATIVE WORK AND THE ANGEL OF LIFE
THE ANGEL OF PEACE AND THE ANGEL OF JOY
THE ANGEL OF POWER AND THE ANGEL OF SUN
THE ANGEL OF LOVE AND THE ANGEL OF WATER
THE ANGEL OF WISDOM AND THE ANGEL OF AIR

These correlations showed the Essenes that when an individual contacts any earthly force he is also in touch with a certain heavenly power. This enabled them to understand how necessary it is to be in perfect harmony with each one of the forces and angels, both in the visible and invisible worlds.

The symbolical Tree of Life made it clear to the people how inseparably they are linked to all the forces, cosmic and terrestrial, and it showed them what their relationship is to each.

For Further Reading:
The Cosmotherapy of the Essenes
The Essene Science of Life
The Essene Book of Asha
Teachings of the Essenes from Enoch to the Dead Sea Scrolls

THE ESSENE COMMUNIONS

The symbolic Tree of Life enabled the Essenes to understand how they were surrounded by forces, or angels, from the visible world of nature and the invisible cosmic world. The Communions show how each of these forces is utilized in man's body and consciousness.

The Communions are said to have been originated by Esnoch, or Enoch, and were again brought forth by Moses to Esrael, the elect of the people, on the two stone tablets he first brought down from Mount Sinai. The second set of tablets he brought down contained the Ten Commandments, the outer teaching, which he gave to the rest of the people, Israel. But the small minority, Esrael, or the Essenes, from that time on, held their communions morning and evening, to the earthly and heavenly forces, regulating their lives according to the inspiration received from them.

The Communions have three immediate objectives.

The first is to make man conscious of the activities of the different forces and forms of energy which surround him and perpetually flow toward him from nature and the cosmos.

The second is to make him aware of the organs and centers within his being which can receive these currents of energy.

The third is to establish a connection between the organs and centers and their corresponding forces so as to absorb, control and utilize each current.

The Essenes knew that man has different bodily systems to absorb the different energies from food, air, water, solar radiations and so on; and they knew that each individual must control and utilize these powers for himself through his own conscious efforts, and that no one could do it for him.

The Communions were practiced each morning and evening, a different earthly force being meditated upon each morning upon arising, and a different heavenly force each evening before retiring, each day of the week. This made a total of fourteen communions during each seven day period.

At each of the Communions the designated force was concentrated upon, contemplated and meditated upon so

41

that its power could be absorbed and consciously utilized in whatever intensity was required.

The Earthly Mother—Saturday Morning

The purpose of this Communion was to establish unity between man's physical organism and the nutritive forces of the earth.

This was accomplished by contemplating the different food substances and realizing that the body is formed of the elements of the earth, and is nourished with those elements through plant life. This teaches the meaning and importance of the natural foods of the earth supplied by the Earthly Mother in harmony with the laws governing terrestrial life. Through this man learns of the paramount role of natural foods in his health and vitality and he becomes conscious of the processes of metabolism within him. He learns, furthermore, how to receive and absorb the powerful energies derived from foods and how to conserve those energies in his body. He thus gradually develops the ability to assimilate perfectly and utilize all the nutritive substances he eats and the energies in them; thus he is able to derive more sustenance from a given amount of food.

This Communion was one of the principal instruments by which the Essenes maintained such remarkable physical health.

The Angel of Earth—Sunday Morning

The Earthly Mother's Angel of Earth was the power of generation and regeneration. A central idea of the Essenes, similar to that of Zarathustra, was to create more and more abundant life. The purpose of the Communion was to transform the biogenic, life-generating powers in life into the regeneration of the human body. They conceived this biogenic power in man to be the same natural force as the generative powers of nature in the top soil, which creates the vegetation of the earth.

This Communion therefore relates to the surface of the earth where things germinate, and to the power of fertility and the glands and organs of generation. It taught the importance of the biogenic, life-generating powers of the soil and of the regenerative force of sexual energy in the glandular system. It made man conscious of all the life-generating forces in and around him, enabling him to be more receptive in absorbing this great power, and mastering, directing, and utilizing it.

The Essenes' extraordinary faculty of self-regeneration was primarily due to their ability to transform biogenic, sexual energy through the practice of this Communion.

The Angel of Life—Monday Morning

This Communion was dedicated to the life, health and vitality of the human organism and that of the whole planet and brought about a dynamic unity between them.

It taught man the role of vitality in his well-being and made him conscious of all the innumerable activities of the life force in and around him, enabling him to direct it to any part of his body in the intensity required.

It gave the Essenes their astonishing ability to absorb life force, especially from fast-growing herbs, trees and forests.

The Angel of Joy—Tuesday Morning

All forms of beauty were joyously contemplated in this Communion in order to make man conscious of the beauties of nature and the joy within himself in every part of his being.

This faculty of absorbing joy from the beauties of nature— sunrises, sunsets, trees, mountains, flowers, colors, aromas and so on—was one of the means by which the Essenes attained the inner harmony and serenity which so impressed their contemporaries.

The Angel of Sun—Wednesday Morning

The Essenes meditated on the Sun as a great living force in terrestrial nature, an ever-present source of energy without which there would be no life on earth, in the ocean or in the atmosphere. They meditated on the effect of solar rays which do not stop at the surface of the body but penetrate the organism at the point where the solar plexus is located, bathing the body and the nervous system in the radiation of the Sun. This point is the oldest unity in the human organism.

The purpose of this Communion was to become receptive to the solar energies and establish a perfect unity between the self and the sun and distribute its power throughout the body. By the Essenes' use of this method certain abnormal conditions were frequently cured in a way that seemed miraculous to the early historians.

The Angel of Water—Thursday Morning

The Essenes considered the circulation of water in nature to correspond to the circulation of the blood in the body. They knew all organisms as well as their foods consist largely of water, which is also essential to life on earth. The perfection of the organism depends upon the quality of the blood, and in like manner the perfection of the physical environment depends upon the quality of the water available.

In this Communion all forms of water were contemplated, rivers, creeks, rain, the sap in trees and plants and so on, establishing as a living reality the unity between the waters of the body and the waters of the planet, thereby making it possible to direct the blood stream to any part of the body or withdraw it at will.

This power enabled the Essenes to cure many conditions otherwise remedied only by long and arduous treatment. It was one of the reasons the Essenes had such complete self mastery and an almost unbelievable resistance to pain.

Angel of Air—Friday Morning

The purpose of this Communion was to make man conscious of the dynamic unity between air and life and that respiration is the link between the organism and the cosmos, that where there is life there is breath, the cessation of one meaning the cessation of the other. Thus the atmosphere in surrounding nature and the air within the body have a stupendous role in health and vitality.

This Communion was accompanied by a certain deep rhythmic breathing enabling the Essenes to absorb specific energies from the atmosphere and establish a correlation of the self and the universe.

These Communions with the Earthly Mother and her Angels were the source from which the Essenes derived their particular way of living, their eating, cold water ablutions, sun bathing, breathing and so on, described by their contemporaries, Josephus, Philo and Pliny, with such astonishment.

For Further Reading:
The Four Volumes of the Essene Gospel of Peace
Essene Communions with the Infinite
The New Fire
I Came Back Tomorrow
The Essene Science of Life
Sexual Harmony
The Conquest of Death
The Essene Science of Fasting & the Art of Sobriety
Ludwig van Beethoven, Prometheus of the Modern World
The Essene Book of Asha
Teachings of the Essenes from Enoch to the Dead Sea Scrolls

THE EVENING COMMUNIONS

In the same way that the seven mornings of the week were devoted to the forces of the visible world, the seven evenings were given to the powers of the invisible realms, or the Angels of the Heavenly Father.

The Heavenly Father—Friday Evening

This Communion with the Heavenly Father, the Creator, the Light, the Ahura Mazda of Zarathustra, was the Essenes' central communion, dedicated to the totality of cosmic laws and to the realization that the universe is a process of continuous creation in which man must take his part by continuing the work of the Creator on earth.

The purpose of the Communion is to teach man the importance of union with the eternal and boundless cosmic ocean of all the superior radiations from all the planets, to make him receptive to these powers so that he may attain cosmic consciousness, enabling him to unite himself with the cosmic currents. Through this he can develop the creative abilities within him to the utmost and learn to use the creative principle in his life and surroundings.

The Essenes knew that only when man does this can he reach his final goal, union with the Heavenly Father, the ultimate aim of all Essenes and the underlying purpose governing all their actions, feelings and thoughts.

The Angel of Eternal Life—Saturday Evening

The Essenes considered that the purpose of the universe can only be eternal life, immortality; and that this can be achieved by man if he progressively creates the preconditions of his advance to higher and higher degrees of his individual evolution. They held that there was no limit to this progress since the cosmos is an inexhaustible store of energies available to man as he perfects his receptive organs and centers.

Through this Communion man can arouse his intuitive knowledge of the eternity of life in the universe and his own unity with this eternal life and the whole cosmic order. Through it he can learn the importance of overcoming gravity in the earthly currents of thought and become conscious of the superior currents' activity and role in the individual's and the planetary evolution.

The Angel of Creative Work—Sunday Evening

This Communion was dedicated to all the great things which have been created by human labor, the great masterpieces of literature, art, science, philosophy and everything man has created as a superstructure on nature, the great values brought forth by previous generations and inherited by the present one.

The purpose of the Communion was to teach the vital importance of creative work and its paramount role in the individual's evolution. It was also to enable him to absorb energies and power from the creative works of mankind, all of its masterpieces, and to use this power in all manifestations of his consciousness.

In the Essene Brotherhoods everyone carried on creative work of some kind, whether in the improvement of himself, the Brotherhood or mankind. The Essenes considered creative work the most adequate expression of love.

The Angel of Peace—Monday Evening

The Communion with the Angel of Peace was dedicated to man's deep inner intuition of peace within himself and with all the infinite universe. In the Essene concept peace is one of the most valuable treasures of man and unless he realizes its true meaning he cannot have spirituality, without which his life can have no meaning. It was held that man's most immediate duty is to create peace within himself and with everything around him; and that the work of peace begins inside himself.

The Essenes utilized all sources of peace in the universe and transmitted them to the world, one manifestation of which was in their universal greeting, "Peace be with you."

The Angel of Power—Tuesday Evening

The Essenes conceived of the whole universe as a cosmic ocean of life in which currents of cosmic power are continually uniting all forms of life on all planets and connecting man with all other organisms.

The Communion made man conscious of these cosmovital forces surrounding him and within him. By becoming receptive to their activity he can absorb them through his nervous system and utilize them in every department of his life.

The Essenes were able to absorb and utilize these currents to a remarkable degree.

The Angel of Love—Wednesday Evening

Love was considered by the Essenes to be the highest creative feeling and they held that a cosmic ocean of love exists everywhere uniting all forms of life, and that life itself is an expression of love.

The purpose of the Communion is to teach man the importance and meaning of these superior currents of feeling in himself and in the surrounding universe; and to make him conscious of and receptive to them as a powerful source of energy and power which he can concentrate and direct in all manifestations of his consciousness.

In the concept of the Essenes, any individual who hurts any form of life outside himself hurts himself equally, because of the dynamic unity of all forms of life in the cosmic ocean of love. The Essenes themselves expressed strong feelings of love to the whole of mankind, near and far, and to all forms of life on earth and in infinite space.

This love which they felt was the cause of their living together in brotherhood communities; it was why they distributed all their surplus of food to the needy and went out of their way to teach the ignorant and heal the sick. They expressed their love through deeds.

This faculty of attracting and sending forth superior currents of feeling was one of the great mystical accomplishments of the Essenes.

The Angel of Wisdom—Thursday Evening

Thought was held by the Essenes to be both a cosmic and a cerebral function. They considered there is a cosmic ocean of thought pervading all space containing all thought, which is the highest and most powerful of all cosmic energies, never perishing and never lost.

By tuning in to all thought currents in the universe and the thought of all great thinkers of the past through communion with the Angel of Wisdom, man developed his ability to create powerful harmonious thought currents and attain intuitive knowledge and wisdom.

Through the application of this Communion the Essenes had great ability to send and receive powerful thought currents.

This Communion with the Angel of Wisdom completes the fourteen Communions of the Essenes. The morning Communions refer to the vitality of the body and their cumulative effect is the gradual strengthening and revitalizing of every organ of the body through the conscious control and direction of earthly forces.

The seven evening Communions are dedicated to the spiritual powers which govern man's higher evolution. Their cumulative effect is the revitalizing of the mind and all the superior forces within the individual, enabling him to receive and become attuned with all the higher oceans of love, life and thought, thus gradually developing all the superior potentialities of his being.

Each Communion of the fourteen represents a certain equilibrium between the person making it and the angel or force communed with.

For Further Reading:
Man in the Cosmic Ocean
Essene Communions with the Infinite
Toward the Conquest of the Inner Cosmos
Creative Work: Karma Yoga
The Art of Study: the Sorbonne Method
Messengers from Ancient Civilizations
The Essene Book of Asha
The Living Buddha
The Zend Avesta of Zarathustra
Teachings of the Essenes from Enoch to the Dead Sea Scrolls

THE NOON CONTEMPLATIONS

A third group of practices was held at noon each day of the week. These were contemplations calling upon the Heavenly Father to send his Angel of Peace to harmonize the different departments of man's life. So important was peace to the Essenes that they had a special teaching concerning it which they called the Sevenfold Peace.

The practice of the fourteen Communions brings about an inner experience or expansion of consciousness enabling the individual to make conscious use of the invisible forces of nature and the cosmos. The Sevenfold Peace shows the practical application of this expanded consciousness in the individual's daily life in its relationship to the different aspects of life.

These Peace Contemplations were practiced in the following order:

FRIDAY NOON—PEACE WITH THE BODY
THURSDAY NOON—PEACE WITH THE MIND
WEDNESDAY NOON—PEACE WITH THE FAMILY
TUESDAY NOON—PEACE WITH HUMANITY
MONDAY NOON—PEACE WITH CULTURE
SUNDAY NOON—PEACE WITH THE EARTHLY MOTHER
SATURDAY NOON—PEACE WITH THE HEAVENLY FATHER

An explanation of these seven departments of the individual's life is given in a subsequent chapter.

Every seventh day, the Essene Sabbath, was consecrated to one of the aspects of peace and communal gatherings were held, separate from the individual contemplations. These gatherings were for the purpose of considering the practical collective application of the particular peace being concentrated upon on that Sabbath.

For Further Reading:
The Essene Code of Life
The Royal Card Game of Asha
Teachings of the Essenes from Enoch to the Dead Sea Scrolls

THE GREAT SABBATH

Every seventh Sabbath was called the Great Sabbath and was dedicated to Peace with the Heavenly Father. This was the transcendental Peace, containing all other aspects of peace. Thus every phase of man's life was given consideration, one after the other.

Such was the Essene pattern of Communion with the cosmic and natural forces and contemplation with the aspects of peace that showed them how to put the forces into practice in their individual lives. We shall not find its equivalent in any other system. It has the wisdom of eight thousand years behind it. It is not merely a form or a ritual; it is a dynamic, intuitive experience. It can establish the unity of mankind.

The Essenes practiced these Communions and Contemplations more than two thousand years ago. We can practice them today.

THE SEVENFOLD PEACE

The Sevenfold Peace of the Essenes was the summation of their inner teaching.

Their Tree of Life and the Communions taught man his relationship with the fourteen forces of the visible and invisible worlds. The Sevenfold Peace explains his relationship to the parts of his own being and to his fellow men, showing how to create peace and harmony in the seven categories of his life.

Harmony to the Essenes meant peace.

They considered that human life can be divided into seven departments: physical, mental, emotional, social, cultural, its relationship with nature and its relationship with the entire cosmos.

Man, it was held, has three bodies that function in each of these departments: an acting body, a feeling body, and a thinking body. The thinking body's highest power is wisdom. The feeling body's highest power is love. The acting body's function is to translate the wisdom of the thinking body and the love of the feeling body into action in an individual's social and cultural worlds and in his utilization of the terrestrial and heavenly forces.

The Sevenfold Peace explains the utilization of these powers and forces with the utmost clarity. Every noon a Peace Contemplation was held with one aspect of peace; and every Sabbath was collectively dedicated to one, the entire cycle covering all phases of life being completed in seven weeks.

Peace With the Body

The word used by the Essenes to indicate the physical body, both in Aramaic and in Hebrew, signified the body's function: to act, to move.

This differs greatly from other concepts. The Greeks, for instance, exalted the body for its esthetic qualities, its proportions and beauty, and were unaware of any deeper purpose. The Romans looked upon the body simply as an instrument of strength and power for conquering nations, planting the Roman eagle in far lands. The medieval Christians disdained the body, considering it the source of all man's troubles, a barrier between man and God.

The Essenes had a much deeper understanding than any of these. They knew that in the acting body, evolving through hundreds of thousands of years, are manifested all the laws of life and the comos; in it is to be found the key to the whole universe.

They studied it in relation to man's whole role in the universe, and their concept of that role was greater than any other which has ever been held. They considered man has three roles: one, of individual evolution; second, a function in regard to the planet on which he lives; and third, a purpose as a unit of the cosmos.

The Essenes knew that man is not an isolated being alone in the universe, but one among other beings on earth and on other planets, all of whom have acting bodies which are evolving even as is man's own. All of these acting bodies are therefore related to each other and affect each other. Every individual's bodily health and vitality is consequently of the utmost importance both to himself and to all other beings on earth and on all other planets.

Those who joined their Brotherhoods were trained to perfect the acting body in all three of its roles, and were taught how to adapt it to the constantly changing field of forces in which it lives and moves.

They were taught the effects on the organism of different foods and the different natural forces of earth, the sun, air and water. They were required to follow certain rituals utilizing these forces, such as starting each day with a cold water ablution and exposing the body once every day to the solar rays. Through practical experience they learned the vitalizing power of working in the fields, orchards and gardens. They learned how disease is created by deviations from the law and how to heal the diseases that result from the deviations.

They learned the material and spiritual value of moderation in all things, and that fasting was a way to regenerate the body and to develop the will, in this way increasing spiritual power.

These practices brought peace and harmony to the acting body.

For Further Reading:
The Chemistry of Youth
The Essene Science of Life
The Book of Living Foods
Scientific Vegetarianism
Treasury of Raw Foods
The Book of Herbs
The Book of Vitamins
The Book of Minerals
Modern Dietetics at a Glance
Healing Waters
Biogenic Reducing: the Wonder Week
Teachings of the Essenes from Enoch to the Dead Sea Scrolls

Peace With the Mind

The quintessence of the teaching in the Sevenfold Peace was concentrated around peace with the mind; mind, in the Essene terminology, being the creator of thought.

The Essenes considered thought to be a superior force, more powerful than the force of either feeling or action, because it is the instigator of both.

The totality of an individual's thoughts was called his thinking body. The totality of the thoughts in all the hundreds of millions of thinking bodies around the surface of the earth forms the planetary thinking body; and the totality of all superior thoughts in the universe forms a cosmic thinking body, or a cosmic ocean of thought.

The Essenes considered an individual's thinking body, like his acting body, has three functions: an individual, a planetary and a cosmic function.

It's individual function is to utilize the power of thought to guide and direct the currents of feeling in the individual's feeling body, and the actions of his acting body. The thinking body can do this because it penetrates through and through the feeling and acting bodies.

The planetary function is to contribute noble and uplifting thoughts to the planetary thinking body. An individual's thoughts form a force field around him comparable to the magnetic field surrounding a magnetic pole. Into this force field the individual's thoughts are constantly pouring and being sent out, and it is also receiving currents of thought from the planetary thinking body of which it is a part. Every individual thus lives, moves, thinks, feels and acts in this surrounding planetary atmosphere of thought, to which he himself is constantly contributing. He is responsible for the thoughts he contributes, for all the thoughts he sends out.

The third function of the thinking body, its cosmic function, is not readily fulfilled. The cosmic ocean of thought, of which the planetary thought atmosphere surrounding the earth is only an infinitesimal part, consists of all the thoughts in the universe superior enough to have become freed of the planetary forces attaching them to their particular planet. Only those highest thought currents which have overcome the planetary gravitation of their planetary atmosphere become united with the infinite cosmic ocean of thought.

This cosmic ocean of thought represents the perfection of the law, the omnipotence of the law and the omnipresence of the law. It has always existed and it always will exist. It is more ancient than any of the existing planets in the solar system, more ancient than the existing solar system itself, or than the galactic or ultra-galactic systems. Eternal and infinite, it directs all the steps of the cosmic and planetary evolution in the infinite cosmic ocean of life.

The cosmic function of each individual's thinking body is to create thoughts of so superior a quality that they can unite with this cosmic ocean of thought.

The Essenes considered that the thinking body is man's highest gift from his Creator. For it, and it alone, gives him the capacity to become conscious of the Law, to understand it, to work in harmony with it, to perceive its manifestations in all his surroundings, in himself, in every cell and molecule of his physical body, in everything that is, and to realize its omnipresence and omnipotence. By becoming conscious of the Law, by understanding it, by acting in harmony with it, man becomes a co-creator with God; there is no greater or higher value in the universe.

Man continually tries to evolve ways to better the conditions in which he lives. But he does this too often without regard for the Law. He seeks peace and harmony by material means, technical evolution, economic systems, not knowing that the conditions of inharmony which he himself has brought into being can never be remedied by material means. The ocean of suffering and inharmony that humanity has created can only be destroyed when mankind sets into motion the law of harmony in his thinking body. Only through complete cooperation with the Law can peace and harmony be brought to the planet.

For Further Reading:
The Evolution of Human Thought
The Dialectical Method of Thinking
Essene Communions with the Infinite
Teachings of the Essenes from Enoch to the Dead Sea Scrolls

Peace With the Family

The third peace of the Essenes, peace with the family, concerns harmony in the feeling body, harmony in the emotions.

By the term family the Essenes meant those in the individual's immediate environment, the people he contacts in his daily life and thought: his family, relatives, friends and associates. According to the Essene tradition, harmony with these people depends upon the feeling body.

The natural function of the feeling body is to express love. Mankind has been told this over and over again by the great Masters, Jesus, Buddha, Zarathustra, Moses and the Prophets.

The feeling body consists of all the currents of feeling and emotions an individual experiences and sends out into the atmosphere about him.

Just as the thinking bodies of all the individuals on the planet create a thought atmosphere around it, so do all the feeling bodies create a planetary feeling atmosphere, invisible and imponerable, but having enormous influence and power. Every feeling and emotion created by an individual becomes a part of the feeling atmosphere of earth, setting up a resonance of co-vibration with all similar feelings in the earth's atmosphere.

If an inferior feeling is sent out, its creator is immediately tuned in to all the similar inferior feelings in the earth's feeling body. He thus opens the gate to a flood of destructive power which rushes in and seizes control of his feelings, and often of his mind, amplifying his own low feelings just as an audio speaker amplifies or intensifies sound.

This destructive force directly affects the individual's physical body. It affects the functioning of the endocrine glands and the whole glandular system. It produces disease cells that lower vitality, shorten life and result in unlimited suffering. It is thus not surprising that statistics of nervous disorders and other diseases are so appalling in spite of all the hospitals, sanitariums, medical organizations, laboratories and the progress of hygiene and medicine.

Through his feeling body man has become an auto-intoxicating automaton, because of his deviation from the law, his acting without knowledge of the law, against it instead of with it.

Through the power of thought man can handle every situation in his life more adequately than through unthinking emotion. But the actions of most people are far more often the expression of impulses in the feeling body than of reasoned thought. This results in a tremendous imbalance in his bodies.

Nature has given man the capacity to think so he may be able to understand its laws and direct his life in harmony with them. Man can reach a far higher degree of evolution through thinking than through living by instinct. So when he continues to let his feeling body be the dominating power in his actions, he not only retards his own evolution but that of the planet.

All the great teachers of humanity through thousands of years have warned man of the consequences of deviation from the law of the feeling body. Buddha pointed out how it results in suffering, suffering for the individual and suffering for humanity.

The Essenes showed that the feeling body can be the most powerful instrument for the production of health, vitality and happiness, and that through its right functioning in expressing love, man can create the kingdom of heaven in and around himself and the whole human family.

For Further Reading:
The Essene Jesus
The Essene Book of Asha
The Essene Code of Life
Essene Communions with the Infinite
Teachings of the Essenes from Enoch to the Dead Sea Scrolls

Peace With Humanity

The fourth peace of the Essenes referred to harmony between groups of people, to social and economic peace. Mankind has never enjoyed social peace in any age in history. Man has always exploited man economically, oppressed him politically, suppressed him by military force. The Essenes knew these injustices were caused by deviations from the law. The very same deviations that produce inharmony in man's personal life, in his acting, thinking and feeling bodies, produce wealth and poverty, masters and slaves, social unrest.

The Essenes regarded both riches and poverty to be the result of deviations from the law.

Great wealth, they considered, is concentrated into the hands of the few because of man's exploitation of man, in one way or another. This has caused misery for both suppressor and suppressed. The many feel hatred and its kindred destructive emotions. This produces fear in the hearts of the exploiters, fear of revolt, fear of losing their possessions, even their lives.

Poverty was held to be an equal deviation from the law. A man is poor because of wrong attitudes of thinking, feeling and acting. He is ignorant of the law and fails to work with the law. The Essenes showed that there is an abundance for everyone of all that a man needs for his use and happiness.

Limitations and over-abundance are both artificial states, deviations from the law. They produce the vicious circle of fear and revolt, a permanent atmosphere of inharmony, affecting the thinking, feeling and acting bodies of both rich and poor, continually creating a state of unrest, war and chaos. This has been the condition throughout recorded history.

The rich and the poor alike suffer the consequences of their deviations.

But a higher and higher understanding of the law can be brought about gradually, the Essenes believed, through teaching and example. They taught a quite opposite way of existence from either poverty or great wealth. They demonstrated in their daily lives that if man lives according to the law, seeks to understand the law and consciously cooperates with it, he will know no lack. He will be able to maintain an all-sided harmony in every act and thought and feeling, and he will find his every need fulfilled.

They demonstrated to humanity that man's daily bread, his food and all his material needs can be acquired without struggle through the knowledge of the law.

Strict rules and regulations were unnecessary for all lived in accord with the law. Order, efficiency and individual freedom existed side by side. The Essenes were extremely practical as well as highly spiritual and intellectual.

Their brotherhoods were partly cooperative. Each member of the group had his own small house and a garden large enough for him to grow whatever he especially desired. But he also took part in communal activities wherever his service might be needed, such as in the pasturing of animals, planting and harvesting of crops most economically grown on an extensive basis.

They had great agricultural proficiency and a thorough knowledge of plant life, soil and climatic conditions. In comparatively desert areas they produced a large variety of fruits and vegetables of the highest quality and in such abundance they periodically had a surplus to distribute to the needy. Their scientific knowledge was such that they could do all of this in a comparatively few hours each day, leaving ample time for their studies and spiritual practices.

Nature was their Bible. They considered gardening educational, a key to the understanding of the entire universe, revealing all its laws, even as does the acting body. They read and studied the great book of nature throughout their lives, in all their brotherhoods, as an inexhaustible source of knowledge, as well as of energy and harmony. When they dug in their gardens and tended their plantings they held communion with the growing things, the trees, sun, soil, rain. From all of these forces they received their education, their pleasure and their recreation.

One of the reasons for their great success was this attitude toward their work. They did not consider it as work but as a means of studying the forces and laws of nature. It was in this that their economic system differed from all others. The vegetables and fruits they produced were only the incidental results of their activities; their real reward was in the knowledge, harmony and vitality they gained to enrich their lives. The Essenes knew it takes many generations to effect changes in people or in mankind as a whole, but they sent out teachers and healers from their brotherhoods whose lives and accomplishments would manifest the truths they taught and little by little increase mankind's understanding and desire to live in accord with the law. The Essene Brotherhood at the Dead Sea for many centuries sent out such teachers as John the Baptist, Jesus and John the Beloved. They warned again and again of the consequences of man's social and economic deviations from the law. Prophet after prophet was sent forth to warn of the dangers incurred by the social injustices that existed then even as they exist today.

The Essenes knew that through the cumulative effect of example and teaching the minority who understand and obey the law will someday grow through the generations to become, finally, the majority of mankind.

Then and then only will mankind know this fourth peace of the Essenes, peace with humanity.

For Further Reading:
Search for the Ageless, Volume Two
Father, Give Us Another Chance
Cosmos, Man and Society
Three Talks
Esperanto Wall Chart
El Minifundio
Teachings of the Essenes from Enoch to the Dead Sea Scrolls

Peace with culture refers to the utilization of the master-pieces of wisdom from all ages, including the present.

The Essenes held that man can take his rightful place in the universe only by absorbing all possible knowledge from the great teachings which have been given forth by masters of wisdom.

According to the Essene traditions these masterpieces represented one third of all knowledge. They considered there are three pathways to the finding of truth. One is the path of intuition which was followed by the mystics and prophets. Another is the pathway of nature, that of the scientist. The third is the pathway of culture, that of great masterpieces of literature and the arts.

The Essenes preserved many precious manuscripts in their brotherhoods which they constantly studied by a method found in no other school of thought in antiquity. They studied them by following the first two pathways to truth: intuition and nature.

Through intuition they endeavored to apprehend the original higher intuition of the master and so awaken their own higher consciousness. Through nature, from which the great masters drew comparisons to express their intuitive knowledge to the masses, the Essenes correlated their own intuitive observations with the teachings of the masters. By this continual comparison between nature, their own intuitions and the great masterpieces of culture, their own individual evolution was advanced.

It was also considered to be every man's duty to acquire the wisdom from these masterpieces so that the experience, knowledge and wisdom already attained by previous genera-tions could be utilized. Without these teachings the progress and evolution of mankind would be much slower than it is, for every generation would have to start all over again from the beginning. In universal culture man has added something new to the planet and so has become a creator, a co-creator with God. Thus he performs his function on the planet by continuing the work of creation.

Universal culture is of great value to humanity from two

other standpoints. First, it represents the highest ideals held by mankind. Second, it represents an all-sided synthesis of knowledge of the problems of life and their right solution. This knowledge was brought forth by highly evolved individuals, masters who had the power to contact the universal sources of knowledge, energy and harmony which exist in the cosmic ocean of thought. Evidence of this contact was their conscious directing of the forces of nature in ways the world today terms miracles. These manifestations of their powers drew about them a limited number of followers who were advanced enough in their own evolution to understand the deeper meaning of the master's teaching. These disciples endeavored to preserve the truths taught by writing down the master's words. This was the origin of all the great masterpieces of universal literature.

The truths in these masterpieces are eternal. They are valid for all time. They come from the one eternal unchanging source of all knowledge. The cosmic and natural laws, nature, man's inner consciousness are the same today as two or ten thousand years ago. Such teachings belong to no one school of thought or religion. The Essenes believed man should study all the great sacred books of humanity, all the great contributions to culture, for they knew all teach the same ageless wisdom and any seeming contradictions come through the one-sidedness of the followers who have attempted to interpret them.

The object of study, they held, is not to add a few additional facts to the store of knowledge an individual already may have. It is to open to him sources of universal truth. They considered that when a man reads a great sacred book of humanity, the symbols of letters and words themselves create in the thinking body powerful vibrations and currents of thought. These vibrations and currents put the individual in touch with the thinking body of the great master who gave forth the truth.

This opens up for the individual a source of knowledge, harmony and power obtainable in no other way. This is the great value, the inner meaning, of the fifth peace of the Essenes.

For Further Reading:
Essene Communions with the Infinite
Books, Our Eternal Companions
Toward the Conquest of the Inner Cosmos
The Art of Study: the Sorbonne Method
The Essene Book of Asha
Ancient America: Paradise Lost
Death of the New World
The Soul of Ancient Mexico
The New Fire
Northern Summer
Ludwig van Beethoven, Prometheus of the Modern World
Teachings of the Essenes from Enoch to the Dead Sea Scrolls

Peace With the Kingdom of the Earthly Mother

The sixth peace teaches harmony with the laws of terrestrial nature, the kingdom of the Earthly Mother. The unity of man and nature is a basic principle of the Essene science of life.

Man is an integral part of nature. He is governed by all the laws and forces of nature. His health, vitality and well-being depend upon his degree of harmony with earth forces; and that of every individual, every nation and the whole of humanity will always be in direct proportion to man's observance of terrestrial laws.

Universal history shows that every nation reached its greatest splendor by following the great law of unity between man and nature. Its vitality and prosperity flourished when the people lived a simple natural life of cooperation with nature. But when the nation or civilization deviates from unity, it inevitably disintegrates and disappears.

This unity of man and nature has never been so heavily transgressed as in the present day. Modern man's building of cities is in entire variance with nature. The city's stone and concrete walls are the symbols of man's separation from nature, of his aggressive way of life with its urges to subjugation of others and to constant competition, one with another. His present centralized, technical and mechanized life creates a chasm separating him from nature, a chasm which never was wider or deeper.

Unity with nature is the foundation of man's existence on the planet. It is the foundation of all economic systems, of all social relationships between groups of people. Without it, the present civilization like those of the past will move toward decline and decay.

This law of unity was held by the Essenes to be the guiding norm for the daily life of man in the material universe.

The idea of unity between man and nature has inspired great thinkers, philosophers and whole systems of thought. Zarathustra taught his followers that it was their duty to maintain the topsoil, to study gardening and all the laws of nature and to collaborate with its forces to improve the entire vegetable kingdom and extend it over the surface of the whole earth. He urged his followers to take an active part in developing every aspect of terrestrial nature, plants, trees, and all their products.

The ideal existence for man, Zarathustra taught, is that of the gardener whose work with the soil, air, sunshine and rain keeps him constantly contacting the forces of nature and studying their laws. Study of this greatest book, the book of nature, Zarathustra considered the first step in creating peace and harmony in the kingdom of the Earthly Mother.

But the unity between man and nature has been given its most complete and poetic expression in the second chapter of the Essene Gospel of Peace in which Jesus borrowed his whole terminology from nature to show that man is an integral part of it. Jesus gave a last warning regarding this unity and the necessity of returning to it.

Man needs today to learn harmony and peace with nature more than in any other age in history. There are enormous regions over the earth where he is letting the precious top-soil deteriorate and disappear. Never before has there been such wholesale destruction of forests, not only in one or two countries but all over the five continents. As a consequence of this lack of cooperation with nature, the desert areas of the world are increasing, drought is more and more frequent, floods periodically inundate the land. There is an unmistakable deterioration of climate: excessive cold, excessive heat and increasing hordes of insect pests damage crops throughout the world. Instead of following the noble tradition of the Essenes, contemporary man fails to recognize the great law of unity and cooperation with nature, and seems bent on denying and destroying his heritage, refusing to read the great open book of nature which reveals all the laws of life and shows the way to ever increasing happiness for man.

The Essene teaching shows the only way of organizing man's life on this planet, the only foundation for a healthy humanity, peace with the kingdom of the Earthly Mother.

For Further Reading:
I Came Back Tomorrow
Cosmos, Man and Society
Teachings of the Essenes from Enoch to the Dead Sea Scrolls

Peace With the Kingdom of the Heavenly Father
This, the seventh peace, includes all other aspects of peace. The kingdom of the Heavenly Father is the universe, the entire cosmos. It is ruled by the One Law, the totality of all laws. The Heavenly Father is the Law. "The Heavenly Father and I are one."

Law is everywhere present. It is behind all that is manifest and all that is unmanifest. A stone falls, a mountain forms, seas flow according to law. In accord with law solar systems arise, evolve and disappear. Ideas, sensations, intuitions come and go in man's consciousness according to law. All that is, concrete or abstract, material or immaterial, visible or invisible, is ruled by law, the One Law.

The Law is formless as a mathematical equation is formless. Yet it contains all knowledge, all love, all power. It eternally manifests all truth and all reality. It is man's teacher and friend, showing him all he must do, and know, and be to evolve to the being which he will someday become. The Law guides man in every problem, through every obstacle, telling him always the perfect solution.

Peace with the Law means peace and harmony with the cosmic ocean of all the cosmic forces in the universe. Through this peace, man makes contact with all the superior currents and radiations from all the planets in cosmic space. Through it he is able to attain realization of his unity with all the forces in the universe, those of earth and those from all other planets in the solar system and all galactic systems.

Through this peace he can unite with all the highest values in the universe. Through this peace is awakened the inner intuition which was followed by the mystics and prophets of all ages. Through this peace man contacts his Creator.

This peace completes man's evolution. It brings him total happiness. It is his final goal.

The Essenes spoke of the three parts of man: the material body, the feeling body and the thinking body. But they were always aware that these three parts were not a division in reality for they are all parts of the one higher body, the spiritual body. And this spiritual body is one with and part of all else in the universe.

The Essenes taught this peace to humanity so that they could overcome all limitations and contact their universal Source, the same Source with which the great masters throughout the ages have united their consciousness when they gave forth their intuitive teachings showing man how to become conscious of the law, understand it, work with it, and manifest it in action.

The kingdom of the Heavenly Father is always open to him. His return to the universal consciousness, universal supply, is always possible. Once he makes the decision to return and puts forth the persistent effort, he can always go back to the Source, his Heavenly Father, from whom he came and from whom he has never in reality been away.

The great peace of the Essenes teaches man how to go back, how to take the final step that unites him with the cosmic ocean of superior radiations of the whole universe and reach complete union with the Heavenly Father, the totality of all law, the One Law.

This was the ultimate aim of all Essenes and governed their every thought, feeling and action. It is the final aim which all mankind will one day achieve.

For Further Reading:
The Essene Gospel of Peace, Books I, II, III and IV
The Discovery of the Essene Gospel of Peace
Essene Communions with the Infinite
The Essene Book of Asha
The Essene Book of Creation
Teachings of the Essenes from Enoch to the Dead Sea Scrolls

Our Essene Way would not be complete without the most important excerpts from Book One of *The Essene Gospel of Peace*. This legendary work has now appeared in 26 languages, and without any commercial advertising, has reached a distribution of almost two million copies.

from the Essene Gospel of Peace. . .

. . .and Jesus answered: "Seek not the law in your scriptures, for the law is life, whereas the scripture is dead. I tell you truly, Moses received not his laws from God in writing, but through the living word. The law is living word of living God to living prophets for living men. In everything that is life is the law written. You find it in the grass, in the tree, in the river, in the mountain, in the birds of heaven, in the fishes of the sea; but seek it chiefly in yourselves. For I tell you truly, all living things are nearer to God than the scripture which is without life. God so made life and all living things that they might by the everliving word teach the laws of the true God to man. God wrote not the laws in the pages of books, but in your heart and in your spirit. They are in your breath, your blood, your bone; in your flesh, your bowels, your eyes, your ears, and in every little part of your body. They are present in the air, in the water, in the earth, in the plants, in the sunbeams, in the depths and in the heights. They all speak to you that you may understand the tongue and the will of the living God. But you shut your eyes that you may not see, and you shut your ears that you may not hear. I tell you truly, that the scripture is the work of man, but life and all its hosts are the work of our God. Wherefore do you not listen to the words of God which are written in His works? And wherefore do you study the dead scriptures which are the work of the hands of men?"

"How may we read the laws of God elsewhere than in the scriptures? Where are they written? Read them to us from there where you see them, for we know nothing else but the scriptures which we have inherited from our forefathers. Tell us the laws of which you speak, that hearing them we may be healed and justified."

Jesus said: "You do not understand the words of life, because you are in death. Darkness darkens your eyes and your ears are stopped with deafness. For I tell you, it profits you not at all that you pore over dead scriptures if by your deeds you deny him who has given you the scriptures. I tell you truly, God and his laws are not in that which you do. They are not in gluttony and in winebibbing, neither in riotous living, nor in lustfulness, nor in seeking after riches, nor yet in hatred of your enemies. For all these things are far from the true God and from his angels. But all these things come from the kingdom of darkness and the lord of all evils. And all these things do you carry in yourselves; and so the word and the power of God enter not into you, because all manner of evil and all manner of abominations have their dwelling in your body and your spirit. If you will that the living God's word and his power may enter you, defile not your body and your spirit; for the body is the temple of the spirit, and the spirit is the temple of God. Purify, therefore, the temple, that the Lord of the temple may dwell therein and occupy a place that is worthy of him.

"And from all temptations of your body and your spirit, coming from Satan, withdraw beneath the shadow of God's heaven.

"Renew yourselves and fast. For I tell you truly, that Satan and his plagues may only be cast out by fasting and by prayer. Go by yourself and fast alone, and show your fasting to no man. The living God shall see it and great shall be your reward. And fast till Beelzebub and all his evils depart from you, and all the angels of our Earthly Mother come and serve you. For I tell you truly, except you fast, you shall never be freed from the power of Satan and from all diseases that come from Satan. Fast and pray fervently, seeking the power of the living God for your healing. While you fast, eschew the Sons of Men and seek our Earthly Mother's angels, for he that seeks shall find.

"Seek the fresh air of the forest and of the fields, and there in the midst of them shall you find the angel of air. Put off your shoes and your clothing and suffer the angel of air to embrace all your body. Then breathe long and deeply, that the angel of air may be brought within you. I tell you truly, the angel of air shall cast out of your body all uncleannesses which defiled it without and within. And thus shall all evil-smelling and unclean things rise out of you, as the smoke of fire curls upwards and is lost in the sea of the air. For I tell you truly, holy is the angel of air, who cleanses all that is unclean and makes all evil-smelling things of a sweet odor. No man may come before the face of God, whom the angel of air lets not pass. Truly, all must be born again by air and by truth, for your body breathes the air of the Earthly Mother, and your spirit breathes the truth of the Heavenly Father.

"After the angel of air, seek the angel of water. Put off your shoes and your clothing and suffer the angel of water to embrace all your body. Cast yourselves wholly into his enfolding arms, and as often as you move the air with your breath, move with your body the water also. I tell you truly, the angel of water shall cast out of your body all uncleannesses which defiled it without and within. And all unclean and evil-smelling things shall flow out of you, even as the uncleannesses of garments washed in water flow away and are lost in the stream of the river. I tell you truly, holy is the angel of water who cleanses all that is unclean and makes all evil-smelling things of a sweet odor. No man may come before the face of God, whom the angel of water lets not pass. In very truth, all must be born again of water and of truth, for your body bathes in the river of earthly life, and your spirit bathes in the river of life everlasting. For you receive your blood from our Earthly Mother and the truth from our Heavenly Father.

"And if afterward there remain within you aught of your past sins and uncleannesses, seek the angel of sunlight. Put off your shoes and your clothing and suffer the angel of sunlight to embrace all your body. Then breathe long and deeply, that the angel of sunlight may be brought within you. And the angel of sunlight shall cast out of your body all evil-smelling and unclean things which defiled it without and within. And all unclean and evil-smelling things shall rise from you, even as the darkness of night fades before the brightness of the rising sun. For I tell

71

you truly, holy is the angel of sunlight who cleans out all uncleannesses and makes all evil-smelling things of a sweet odor. None may come before the face of God, whom the angel of sunlight lets not pass. Truly, all must be born again of sun and of truth, for your body basks in the sunlight of the Earthly Mother, and your spirit basks in the sunlight of truth of the Heavenly Father.

"The angels of air and of water and of sunlight are brethren. They were given to the Son of Man that they might serve him, and that he might go always from one to the other.

"Holy, likewise, is their embrace. They are indivisible children of the Earthly Mother, so do not you put asunder those whom earth and heaven have made one. Let these three brother angels enfold you every day and let them abide with you through all your fasting.

"It was said to you: 'Honor thy father and thy mother that thy days may be long upon this earth.' But I say to you, Sons of Man: Honor your Earthly Mother and keep all her laws, that your days may be long on this earth, and honor your Heavenly Father that eternal life may be yours in the heavens. For the Heavenly Father is a hundred times greater than all fathers by seed and by blood, and greater is the Earthly Mother than all mothers by the body. And dearer is the Son of Man in the eyes of his Heavenly Father and of his Earthly Mother than are children in the eyes of their fathers by seed and by blood and of their mothers by the body. And more wise are the words and laws of your Heavenly Father and of your Earthly Mother than the words and the will of all fathers by seed and by blood, and of all mothers by the body. And of more worth also is the inheritance of your Heavenly Father and of your Earthly Mother, the everlasting kingdom of earthly and heavenly life, than all the inheritances of your fathers by seed and by blood, and of your mothers by the body.

"And your true brothers are all those who do the will of your Heavenly Father and of your Earthly Mother, and not your brothers by blood. I tell you truly, that your true brothers in the will of the Heavenly Father and of the Earthly Mother will love you a thousand times more than your brothers by blood. For since the days of Cain and Abel, when brothers by blood transgressed the will of God, there is no true brotherhood by blood. And brothers do unto brothers as do strangers. Therefore, I say to you, love your true brothers in the will of God a thousand times more than your brothers by blood.

"FOR YOUR HEAVENLY FATHER IS LOVE.
"FOR YOUR EARTHLY MOTHER IS LOVE.
"FOR THE SON OF MAN IS LOVE.
"It is by love that the Heavenly Father and the Earthly Mother and the Son of Man become one. For the spirit of the Son of Man was created from the spirit of the Heavenly Father, and his body from the body of the Earthly Mother. Become, therefore, perfect as the spirit of your Heavenly Father and the body of your Earthly Mother are perfect.

And so love your Heavenly Father, as he loves your spirit. And so love your Earthly Mother, as she loves your body. And so love your true brothers, as your Heavenly Father and your Earthly Mother love them. And then your Heavenly Father shall give you his holy spirit, and your Earthly Mother shall give you her holy body. And then shall the Sons of Men like true brothers give love one to another, the love which they received from their Heavenly Father and from their Earthly Mother; and they shall all become comforters one of another. And then shall disappear from the earth all evil and sorrow, and there shall be love and joy upon earth. And then shall the earth be like the heavens, and the kingdom of God shall come. And then shall come the Son of Man in all his glory, to inherit the kingdom of God. And then shall the Sons of Men divide their divine inheritance, the kingdom of God. For the Sons of Man live in the Heavenly Father and in the Earthly Mother, and the Heavenly Father and the Earthly Mother live in them. And then with the kingdom of God shall come the end of the times. For the Heavenly Father's love gives to all life everlasting in the kingdom of God. For love is eternal. Love is stronger than death.

"And now I speak to you in the living tongue of the living God, through the holy spirit of our Heavenly Father. There is none yet among you that can understand all of this which I speak. He who expounds to you the scriptures speaks to you in a dead tongue of dead men, through his diseased and mortal body. Him, therefore, can all men understand, for all men are diseased and all are in death. No one sees the light of life. Blind man leads blind on the dark paths of sins, diseases and sufferings; and at the last all fall into the pit of death.

"I am sent to you by the Father, that I may make the light of life to shine before you. The light lightens itself and the darkness, but the darkness knows only itself, and knows not the light. I have still many things to say to you, but you cannot bear them yet. For your eyes are used to the darkness, and the full light of the Heavenly Father would make you blind. Therefore, you cannot yet understand that which I speak to you concerning the Heavenly Father who sent me to you. Follow, therefore, first, only the laws of your Earthly Mother, of which I have told you. And when her angels shall have cleansed and renewed your bodies and strengthened your eyes, you will be able to bear the light of our Heavenly Father. When you can gaze on the brightness of the noonday sun with unflinching eyes, you can then look upon the blinding light of our Heavenly Father, which is a thousand times brighter than the brightness of a thousand suns. But how should you look upon the blinding light of your Heavenly Father, when you cannot even bear the shining of the blazing sun? Believe me, the sun is as the flame of a candle beside the sun of truth of the Heavenly Father. Have but faith, therefore, and hope, and love. I tell you truly, you shall not want your reward. If you believe in my words, you believe in him who sent me, who is the lord of all, and with whom all things are possible.

For what is impossible with men, all these things are possible with God. If you believe in the angels of the Earthly Mother and do her laws, your faith shall sustain you and you shall never see disease. Have hope also in the love of your Heavenly Father, for he who trusts in him shall never be deceived, nor shall he ever see death.

"Love one another, for God is love, and so shall his angels know that you walk in his paths. And then shall all the angels come before your face and serve you. And Satan with all sins, diseases and uncleannesses shall depart from your body. Go, eschew your sins; repent yourselves; baptize yourselves; that you may be born again and sin no more."

Then Jesus rose. But all else remained sitting, for every man felt the power of his words. And then the full moon appeared between the breaking clouds and folded Jesus in its brightness. And sparks flew upward from his hair, and he stood among them in the moonlight, as though he hovered in the air. And no man moved, neither was the voice of any heard. And no one knew how long a time had passed, for time stood still.

Then Jesus stretched out his hands to them and said: "Peace be with you." And so he departed, as a breath of wind sways the green of trees.

And for a long while yet the company sat still and then they woke in the silence, one man after another, like as from a long dream. But none would go, as if the words of him who had left them ever sounded in their ears. And they sat as though they listened to some wondrous music.

But at last one, as it were a little fearfully, said: "How good it is to be here." Another: "Would that this night were everlasting." And others: "Would that he might be with us always." "Of truth he is God's messenger, for he planted hope within our hearts." And no man wished to go home, saying: "I go not home where all is dark and joyless. Why should we go home where no one loves us?"

And they spoke on this wise, for they were almost all poor, lame, blind, maimed, beggars, homeless, despised in their wretchedness, who were only borne for pity's sake in the houses where they found a few days' refuge. Even certain, who had both home and family, said: "We also will stay with you." For every man felt that the words of him who was gone bound the little company with threads invisible. And all felt that they were born again. They saw before them a shining world, even when the moon was hidden in the clouds. And in the hearts of all blossomed wondrous flowers of wondrous beauty, the flowers of joy.

And when the bright sunbeams appeared over the earth's rim, they all felt that it was the sun of the coming kingdom of God. And with joyful countenances they went forth to meet God's angels.

And it was by the bed of a stream, many sick fasted and prayed with God's angels for seven days and seven nights. And great was their reward, because they followed Jesus' words. And with the passing of the seventh day, all their pains left them. And when the sun rose over the earth's rim they saw Jesus coming towards them from the mountain, with the brightness of the rising sun about his head.

"Peace be with you."

And they said no word at all, but only cast themselves down before him, and touched the hem of his garment in token of their healing.

"Give thanks not to me, but to your Earthly Mother, who sent you her healing angels. Go, and sin no more, that you may never again see disease. And let the healing angels become your guardians."

But they answered him: "Whither should we go, Master, for with you are the words of eternal life? Tell us, what are the sins which we must shun, that we may nevermore see disease?"

Jesus answered: "Be it so according to your faith," and he sat down among them, saying:

"It was said to them of old time, 'Honor thy Heavenly Father and thy Earthly Mother, and do their commandments, that thy days may be long upon the earth.' And next afterward was given this commandment, 'Thou shalt not kill,' for life is given to all by God, and that which God has given, let not man take away. For I tell you truly, from one Mother proceeds all that lives upon the earth. Therefore, he who kills, kills his brother. And from him will the Earthly Mother turn away, and will pluck from him her quickening breasts. And he will be shunned by her angels, and Satan will have his dwelling in his body. And the flesh of slain beasts in his body will become his own tomb. For I tell you truly, he who kills, kills himself, and whoso eats the flesh of slain beasts, eats of the body of death. For in his blood every drop of their blood turns to poison; in his breath their breath to stink; in his flesh their flesh to boils; in his bones their bones to chalk; in his bowels their bowels to decay; in his eyes their eyes to scales; in his ears their ears to waxy issue. And their death will become his death. For only in the service of your Heavenly Father are your debts of seven years forgiven in seven days. But Satan forgives you nothing and you must pay him for all. 'Eye for eye, tooth for tooth, hand for hand, foot for foot; burning for burning; wound for wound;' life for life, death for death. For the wages of sin is death. Kill not, neither eat the flesh of your innocent prey, lest you become the slaves of Satan. For that is the path of sufferings, and it leads unto death. But do the will of God, that his angels may serve you on the way of life. Obey, therefore, the words of God: 'Behold, I have given you every herb bearing seed, which is upon the face of all the earth, and every tree, in the which is the fruit of a tree yielding seed; to you it shall be for meat. And to every beast of the earth, and to every fowl of the air, and to everything that creepeth upon the earth, wherein there is breath of life, I give every green herb for meat. Also the milk of everything that moveth and that liveth upon earth shall be meat for you; even as the green herb have I given unto them, so I give their milk unto you. But flesh, and the blood which quickens it, shall ye not eat.

"For I tell you truly, man is more than the beast. But he who kills a beast without a cause, though the beast attack him not, through lust for slaughter, or for its flesh, or for its hide, or yet for its tusks, evil is the deed which he does, for he is turned into a wild beast himself. Wherefore is his end also as the end of the wild beasts."

"And when you come before the face of God, his angels bear witness for you with your good deeds. And God sees your good deeds written in your bodies and in your spirits, and rejoices in his heart. He blesses your body and your spirit and all your deeds, and gives you for a heritage his earthly and heavenly kingdom, that in it you may have life everlasting. Happy is he who can enter into the kingdom of God, for he shall never see death."

Then another said: "Moses, the greatest in Israel, suffered our forefathers to eat the flesh of clean beasts, and forbade only the flesh of unclean beasts. Why, therefore, do you forbid us the flesh of all beasts? Which law comes from God? That of Moses or your law?"

And Jesus answered: "God gave, by Moses, ten commandments to your forefathers. 'These commandments are hard,' said your forefathers, and could not keep them. When Moses saw this, he had compassion on his people, and would not that they perish. And then he gave them ten times ten commandments, less hard, that they might follow them. I tell you truly, if your forefathers had been able to keep the ten commandments of God, Moses would never had need of his ten times ten commandments. For he whose feet are strong as the mountain of Zion, needs no crutches; but he whose limbs do shake, gets further having crutches, than without them. And Moses said to the Lord: 'My heart is filled with sorrow, for my people will be lost. For they are without knowledge, and are not able to understand thy commandments. They are as little children who cannot yet understand their father's words. Suffer, Lord, that I give them other laws, that they may not perish. If they may not be with thee, Lord, let them not be against thee; that they may sustain themselves, and when the time has come, and they are ripe for thy words, reveal to them thy laws.' For that did Moses break the two tablets of stone whereon were written the ten commandments, and he gave them ten times ten in their stead. And of these ten times ten the Scribes and Pharisees have made a hundred times ten commandments. And they have laid unbearable burdens on your shoulders, that they do not themselves carry. For the more nigh are the commandments to God, the less do we need; and the farther they are from God, then the more do we need. Wherefore are the laws of the Pharisees and Scribes innumerable; the laws of the Son of Man seven; of the angels three; and of God one.

"Therefore, I teach you only those laws which you can understand, that you may become men, and follow the seven laws of the Son of Man. Then will the angels also reveal their laws to you, that God's holy spirit may descend upon you, and lead you to his law."

And all were astonished at his wisdom, and asked him: "Continue, Master, and teach us all the laws which we can receive."

And Jesus continued: "God commanded your forefathers: 'Thou shalt not kill.' But their heart was hardened and they killed. Then Moses desired that at least they should not kill men, and he suffered them to kill beasts. And then the heart of your forefathers was hardened yet more, and they killed men and beasts likewise. But I do say to you: Kill neither men, nor beasts, nor yet the food which goes into your mouth. For if you eat living food, the same will quicken you, but if you kill your food, the dead food will kill you also. For life comes only from life, and from death comes always death. For everything which kills your foods, kills your bodies also. And everything which kills your bodies kills your souls also. And your bodies become what your foods are, even as your spirits, likewise, become what your thoughts are. You shall live only by the fire of life, and prepare not your foods with the fire of death, which kills your foods, your bodies and your souls also."

"Master, where is the fire of life?" asked some of them.

"In you, in your blood and in your bodies."

"And the fire of death?" asked others.

"It is the fire which blazes outside your body, which is hotter than your blood. With that fire of death you cook your foods in your homes and in your fields. I tell you truly, it is the same fire which destroys your foods and your bodies, even as the fire of malice, which ravages your thoughts, ravages your spirits. For your body is that which you eat, and your spirit is that which you think. Eat nothing, therefore, which a stronger fire than the fire of life has killed. Wherefore, prepare and eat all fruits of trees, and all grasses of the fields, and all milk of beasts good for eating. For all these are fed and ripened by the fire of life; all are the gift of the angels of our Earthly Mother. But eat nothing to which only the fire of death gives savor, for such is of Satan."

"How should we cook our daily bread without fire, Master?" asked some with great astonishment.

"Let the angels of God prepare your bread. Moisten your wheat, that the angel of water may enter it. Then set it in the air, that the angel of air also may embrace it. And leave it from morning to evening beneath the sun, that the angel of sunshine may descend upon it. And the blessing of the three angels will soon make the germ of life to sprout in your wheat. For the angels of water, of air, and of sunshine fed and ripened the wheat in the field, and they, likewise, must prepare also your bread. And the same sun which, with the fire of life, made the wheat to grow and ripen, must cook your bread with the same fire. For the fire of the sun gives life to the wheat, to the bread, and to the body. But the fire of death kills the wheat, the bread, and the body. And the living angels of the living God serve only living men. For God is the God of the living, and not the God of the dead.

"So eat always from the table of God: the fruits of the trees, the grain and grasses of the field, the milk of beasts, and the honey of bees. For everything beyond these is of Satan, and leads by the way of sins and of diseases unto death. But the foods which you eat from the abundant table of God give strength and youth to your body, and you will never see disease. For the table of God fed Methuselah of old, and I tell you truly, if you live even as he lived, then will the God of the living give you also long life upon the earth as was his.

"For I tell you truly, the God of the living is richer than all the rich of the earth, and his abundant table is richer than the richest table of feasting of all the rich upon the earth. Eat, therefore, all your life at the table of our Earthly Mother, and you will never see want. And when you eat at her table, eat all things even as they are found on the table of the Earthly Mother. Cook not, neither mix all things one with another, lest your bowels become as steaming bogs. For I tell you truly, this is abominable in the eyes of the Lord.

"Take heed, therefore, and defile not with all kinds of abominations the temple of your bodies. Be content with two or three sorts of food, which you will find always upon the table of our Earthly Mother. And desire not to devour all things which you see round about you. For I tell you truly, if you mix together all sorts of food in your body, then the peace of your body will cease, and endless war will rage in you. And it will be blotted out even as homes and kingdoms divided against themselves work their own destruction. For your God is the God of peace, and does never help division. Arouse not, therefore, against you the wrath of God, lest he drive you from his table, and lest you be compelled to go to the table of Satan, where the fire of sins, of diseases, and of death will corrupt your body.

"And when you eat, never eat unto fullness. Flee the temptations of Satan, and listen to the voice of God's angels. For Satan and his power tempt you always to eat more and more. But live by the spirit, and resist the desires of the body. And your fasting is always pleasing in the eyes of the angels of God. So give heed to how much you have eaten when your body is sated, and always eat less by a third. Then will the angels of God serve you always, and you will never fall into the bondage of Satan and of his diseases. Trouble not the work of the angels in your body by eating often. For I tell you truly, he who eats more than twice in the day does in him the work of Satan. And the angels of God leave his body, and soon Satan will take possession of it. Eat only when the sun is highest in the heavens, and again when it is set. And you will never see disease, for such finds favor in the eyes of the Lord. The angels will rejoice in your body, and your days will be long upon the earth, for this is pleasing in the eyes of the Lord. Eat always when the table of God is served before you, and eat always of that which you find upon the table of God. For I tell you truly, God knows well what your body needs, and when it needs.

"Happy and wise are they that eat only at the table of God, and eschew all the abominations of Satan. Eat not unclean foods brought from far countries, but eat always that which your trees bear. For your God knows well what is needful for you, and where and when. And he gives to all peoples of all kingdoms for food that which is best for each. Eat not as the heathen do, who stuff themselves in haste, defiling their bodies with all manner of abominations.

"For the power of God's angels enters into you with the living food which the Lord gives you from his royal table. And when you eat, have above you the angel of air, and below you the angel of water. Breathe long and deeply at all your meals, that the angel of air may bless your repasts. And chew well your food with your teeth, that it become water, and that the angel of water turn it into blood in your body. And eat slowly, as it were a prayer you make to the Lord. For I tell you truly, the power of God enters into you, if you eat after this manner at his table. For the table of the Lord is as an altar, and he who eats at the table of God, is in a temple. For I tell you truly, the body of the Sons of Man is turned into a temple, and their inwards into an altar, if they do the commandments of God. Wherefore, put naught upon the altar of the Lord when your spirit is vexed, neither think upon any one with anger in the temple of God. And enter only into the Lord's sanctuary when you feel in yourselves the call of his angels, for all that you eat in sorrow, or in anger, or without desire, becomes a poison in your body. For the breath of Satan defiles all these. Place with joy your offerings upon the altar of your body, and let all evil thoughts depart from you when you receive into your body the power of God from his table. And never sit at the table of God before he call you by the angel of appetite.

"Rejoice, therefore, always with God's angels at their royal table, for this is pleasing to the heart of the Lord. And your life will be long upon the earth, for the most precious of God's servants will serve you all your days: the angel of joy.

"And forget not that every seventh day is holy and consecrated to God. On six days feed your body with the gifts of the Earthly Mother, but on the seventh day sanctify your body for your Heavenly Father. And on the seventh day eat not any earthly food, but live only upon the words of God. And be all the day with the angels of the Lord in the kingdom of the Heavenly Father. And on the seventh day let the angels of God build the kingdom of the heavens in your body, as you labor for six days in the kingdom of the Earthly Mother. And let not food trouble the work of the angels in your body throughout the seventh day. And God will give you long life upon earth, that you may have life everlasting in the kingdom of the heavens. For I tell you truly, if you see not diseases any more upon the earth, you will live for ever in the kingdom of the heavens.

"And God will send you each morning the angel of sunshine to

79

wake you from your sleep. Therefore, obey your Heavenly Father's summons, and lie not idle in your beds, for the angels of air and water await you already without. And labor all day long with the angels of the Earthly Mother that you may come to know them and their works ever more and more well. But when the sun is set, and your Heavenly Father sends you his most precious angel, sleep, then take your rest, and be all the night with the angel of sleep. And then will your Heavenly Father send you his unknown angels, that they may be with you the livelong night. And the Heavenly Father's unknown angels will teach you many things concerning the kingdom of God, even as the angels that you know of the Earthly Mother, instruct you in the things of her kingdom. For I tell you truly, you will be every night the guests of the kingdom of your Heavenly Father, if you do his commandments. And when you wake up upon the morrow, you will feel in you the power of the unknown angels. And your Heavenly Father will send them to you every night, that they may build your spirit, even as every day the Earthly Mother sends you her angels, that they may build your body. For I tell you truly, if in the daytime your Earthly Mother folds you in her arms, and in the night the Heavenly Father breathes his kiss upon you, then will the Sons of Men become the Sons of God.

"Shun all that is too hot and too cold. For it is the will of your Earthly Mother that neither heat nor cold should harm your body. And let not your bodies become either hotter or colder than as God's angels warm or cool them. And if you do the commandments of the Earthly Mother, then as oft as your body becomes too hot, will she the angel of coolness to cool you, and as oft as your body becomes too cold, will she send you the angel of heat to warm you again.

"Follow the example of all the angels of the Heavenly Father and of the Earthly Mother, who work day and night, without ceasing, upon the kingdoms of the heavens and of the earth. Therefore, receive also into yourselves the strongest of God's angels, the angel of deeds, and work all together upon the kingdom of God. Follow the example of the running water, the wind as it blows, the rising and setting of the sun, the growing plants and trees, the beasts as they run and gambol, the wane and waxing of the moon, the stars as they come and go again; all these do move, and do perform their labors. For all which has life does move, and only that which is dead is still. And God is the God of the living, and Satan that of the dead. Serve, therefore, the living God, that the eternal movement of life may sustain you, and that you may escape the eternal stillness of death. Work, therefore, without ceasing, to build the kingdom of God, lest you be cast into the kingdom of Satan. For eternal joy abounds in the living kingdom of God, but still sorrow darkens the kingdom of death of Satan. Be, therefore, true Sons of your Earthly Mother and of your Heavenly Father, that you fall not as slaves of Satan. And your Earthly Mother and Heavenly Father will send you their angels to teach, to love, and to serve you.

And their angels will write the commandments of God in your head, in your heart, and in your hands, that you may know, feel, and do God's commandments.

"And pray every day to your Heavenly Father and Earthly Mother, that your soul become as perfect as your Heavenly Father's holy spirit is perfect, and that your body become as perfect as the body of your Earthly Mother is perfect. For if you understand, feel, and do the commandments, then all for which you pray to your Heavenly Father and your Earthly Mother will be given you. For the wisdom, the love, and the power of God are above all.

"After this manner, therefore, pray to your Heavenly Father: Our Father which art in heaven, hallowed be thy name. Thy kingdom come. Thy will be done on earth as it is in heaven. Give us this day our daily bread. And forgive us our debts, as we forgive our debtors. And lead us not into temptation, but deliver us from evil. For thine is the kingdom, the power, and the glory, for ever. Amen.

"And after this manner pray to your Earthly Mother: Our Mother which art upon earth, hallowed be thy name. Thy kingdom come, and thy will be done in us, as it is in thee. As thou sendest every day thy angels, send them to us also. Forgive us our sins, as we atone all our sins against thee. And lead us not into sickness, but deliver us from all evil, for thine is the earth, the body, and the health. Amen."

And they all prayed together with Jesus to the Heavenly Father and to the Earthly Mother.

And afterwards Jesus spoke thus to them: "Even as your bodies have been reborn through the Earthly Mother's angels, may your spirit, likewise, be reborn through the angels of the Heavenly Father. Become, therefore, true Sons of your Father and of your Mother, and true Brothers of the Sons of Men. Till now you were at war with your Father, with your Mother, and with your Brothers. And you have served Satan. From today live at peace with your Heavenly Father, and with your Earthly Mother, and with your Brothers, the Sons of Men. And fight only against Satan, lest he rob you of your peace. I give the peace of your Earthly Mother to your body, and the peace of your Heavenly Father to your spirit. And let the peace of both reign among the Sons of Men.

"Come to me, all that are weary, and that suffer in strife and affliction! For my peace will strengthen you and comfort you. For my peace is exceeding full of joy. Wherefore do I always greet you after this manner: 'Peace be with you!' Do you always, therefore, so greet one another, that upon your body may descend the peace of your Earthly Mother, and upon your spirit the peace of your Heavenly Father. And then will you find peace also among yourselves, for the kingdom of God is within you. And now return to your Brothers with whom hitherto you were at war, and give your peace to them also. For happy are they that strive for peace, for they will find the peace of

God. Go, and sin no more. And give to every one your peace, even as I have given my peace unto you. For my peace is of God. Peace be with you."

And he left them.

And his peace descended upon them; and in their heart the angel of love, in their head the wisdom of law, and in their hands the power of rebirth, they went forth among the Sons of Men, to bring the light of peace to those that warred in darkness.

And they parted, wishing, one to another:

"PEACE BE WITH YOU."

BIOGENIC LIVING

CREDO
of the International Biogenic Society

We believe that our most precious possession is Life.

We believe we shall mobilize all the forces of Life against the forces of death.

We believe that mutual understanding leads toward mutual cooperation; that mutual cooperation leads toward Peace; and that Peace is the only way of survival for mankind.

We believe that we shall preserve instead of waste our natural resources, which are the heritage of our children.

We believe that we shall avoid the pollution of our air, water, and soil, the basic preconditions of Life.

We believe we shall preserve the vegetation of our planet: the humble grass which came fifty million years ago, and the majestic trees which came twenty million years ago, to prepare our planet for mankind.

We believe we shall eat only fresh, natural, pure, whole foods, without chemicals ånd artificial processing.

We believe we shall live a simple, natural, creative life, absorbing all the sources of energy, harmony and knowledge, in and around us.

We believe that the improvement of life and mankind on our planet must start with individual efforts, as the whole depends on the atoms composing it.

We believe in the Fatherhood of God, the Motherhood of Nature, and the Brotherhood of Man.

—composed in Paris in 1928 by Romain Rolland and Edmond Bordeaux Székely.

WHY BIOGENIC LIVING?

In Greek mythology, Anteus was the son of Gaea, the Earth, and drew invincible power from contact with her. Our modern Anteus, twentieth century man, is also the child of Mother Earth—Nature. In the Greek legend, Hercules, the most powerful being on earth, was unable to defeat Anteus, because each time he threw him to the ground, Anteus immediately gained power from his Mother and rose up again and again against the terrible Hercules. And, like Anteus, while we live in and by Nature, we too are strong and invincible. But the legend goes on to tell how finally Hercules prevented Anteus from returning to his Mother, the Earth, and was able to strangle him, weakened and bereft of his earth-given power.

All of us today are Anteus in the twentieth century, fighting a losing battle against the present-day mad monster, Giant Centralized Industry (American, Russian, German, Japanese, it does not matter—if it is giant, centralized, and industry) which, obsessed by the evil, mad spirit of greed and competition, is squandering all our natural resources, spending recklessly the unredeemable capital of mankind in order to manufacture on an enormous scale an unbiodegradable, unrecyclable inundation of unnecessary luxuries, creating with dizzying speed an alarmingly increasing pollution of all our vital sources of life—our atmosphere, our oceans, rivers and lakes, our soil, fields and forests—destroying forever thousands of forms of life created millions of years ago on our planet.

Very soon this insatiable monster-of-monsters, Giant Centralized Industry, will sever us completely from Nature which covers Mother Earth and strangle us, tossing our anemic, sick and weak bodies on the heap of a planet-size mountain of life-destroying poisonous rubble.

We must hope that we can still avoid the fate of Anteus, and that we may, by united effort, enchain the twentieth century Hercules, Giant Centralized Industry, hungrily devouring our planet, by creating a new life style of decentralized, simple, natural, creative, healthy, and meaningful living, uniting all the forces of Life against the forces of death.

In this decisive battle of the forces of Life against the forces of death, we biogenists have an additional and perhaps the most important contribution to the side of Life. This contribution is the biogenic principle of immediate reorganization of life in our own individual environment around the fundamental, biogenic, life-generating primeval power as manifest in immediately-created, new living organisms, with which we are phylogenetically united through our primeval history of millions of years.

We do not have to stand idly by until our conservationist and environmentalist brothers-in-arms will have (we hope) triumphed over the Giant Technological Monster. We can do vitally important things right now in our own individual lives, beginning with a total boycott of the Monster—refusing to use his biocidic products which he is trying to push down our throats by relentless, idiotic and stultifying advertising on television, radio, and other media forms, trying to make us believe that his false luxuries, his plastic and chemicalized junk, are our necessities.

There are many ways, all possible to put into immediate practice, by which we can start to cut through the net of meaningless, harmful, suicidal life-styles surrounding us, and return to our real, basic, natural needs—to our primeval sources of energy, harmony and knowledge.

This is why we need the blessings of Biogenic Living. This is the reason for this book: to teach us who stand at the cross-roads of Life and Death at the end of the twentieth century how to reorganize our lives into new, creative, meaningful ways of daily living: to each become an active point in the universe; to make it possible through example and education that the end of the twentieth century shall not necessarily become the END.

Editor's Note: Edmond Bordeaux Szekely wrote this chapter in 1977. In 1989, his diagnosis and prognosis of our planet's condition has turned out to be devastatingly accurate, and his call for immediate remedial action even more urgent, if we are to avoid the unthinkable, and lose our precious, irreplaceable home—our Earth.

For Further Reading:
Brother Tree
I Came Back Tomorrow
Father, Give Us Another Chance

BIOGENIC LIVING IN WORLD PERSPECTIVES
VITAL SOLUTIONS TO VITAL NEEDS

I have been asked many times why our Biogenic Movement— more correctly, the Essene Way of Biogenic Living—is so successful, and why it has so many enthusiastic followers all over the world.

The answer is at the same time very simple and very complex. The problems of the world suddenly and cumulatively acquired such pressing urgency in so many complex aspects, that due to the vital urgency to find solutions for them, the United Nations was forced to hold ten extraordinary World Conferences, inviting delegates from every nation of the world to deal with these most immediate and actual problems of planet Earth, in search of solutions.

The Essene Way of Biogenic Living has provided these solutions and advocated them for a long time. Our movement has always been the forerunner in these ten fields, recalling the ageless statement of Auguste Compte: "Savoir c'est Prévoir"—to know is to foresee.

Let us examine briefly these ten vital and urgent needs facing mankind today. Without satisfying these needs, our Earth has not much chance to survive.

I. Disarmament and World Peace, the basic goal of the United Nations.

No one will disagree that the most burning immediate problems on earth today are the inevitable proliferation of nuclear armaments combined with famine, starvation, unemployment, substandard living conditions, increasing crime and terrorism, and worldwide emotional immaturity, resulting in all forms of violence. Undoubtedly, the threat of nuclear holocaust is the most urgent of these, for the simple reason that the other problems will have no meaning if human life does not exist on this planet. And this paramount danger cannot be solved by SALT agreements, international conferences, or official visits between heads of state, because the solution can never come from without— it cannot be enforced or imposed from the outside. As the Essene teachings have maintained from time immemorial, peace must start from deep within every one of us, as the position of the whole depends on the position of the atoms composing it. This is why the Sevenfold Peace of the Essenes is the foundation of all things.*

The Sevenfold Peace is sevenfold only in its explanation; in its practice and application it forms a single dynamic unity—an all-sided program of daily living. The Sevenfold Peace can be achieved only by ourselves and through our own efforts; it is impossible to attain in any other way, by laws, conventions, or enforcements in our chaotic world. Unless we understand this, we will continue to waste tremendous energy, time and labor, without achieving *real* peace in and around us.

*See *Teachings of the Essenes, from Enoch to the Dead Sea Scrolls,* by Edmond Bordeaux Szekely, available from the International Biogenic Society.

Unless all of us make relentless efforts to carry this Sevenfold Peace of the Essenes to our immediate and general environment, there will be no hope of survival for mankind.

II. The United Nations World Conference in Stockholm on the Environment.

Multinational corporations, industries, unions, and governments, all the time growing larger and more centralized, all with a humanless face, are destroying our irreplaceable planetary resources and increasingly polluting our vital elements of air, water, and soil. The waste of our resources is leading toward inevitable bankruptcy in energy, and to intolerable saturation levels of pollution, creating unacceptable stress on our environment and making life impossible on our planet.

Well, it is evident that the Essene Way of Biogenic Living is the only safe and complete solution to these problems, as our books, *The Chemistry of Youth* and *The Tender Touch* so vividly demonstrate.

III. The United Nations World Conference in Rome on Food.

Half of our world's population is underfed. At least 150 million children each year are born with physical or mental defects because of malnutrition. And worse is on its way. In a few years, the hungry nations will be short by almost 100 million tons of grain, even in good crop years. The great majority of mankind is faced with ruinous hunger. Will these hundreds of millions starve to death while we in surplus-food countries suffer and strugle with problems caused by excessive eating?

In our books, *The Ecological Health Garden* and *The Chemistry of Youth,* we demonstrated that everybody, even those living in a single room, can harvest sprouts 365 times a year, and tender baby greens 40 times a year. Biogenic Living has opened new frontiers in food self-sufficiency, in light of its universal practicality. Here again, we must start with the individual, and education is our salvation. We want you to cooperate by becoming members of the International Biogenic Society in order to be able to carry out this mission in proportion with our material capacity. Join us by spreading our literature in our own environment as much as possible. Time is short. The problem is vital. And we have the solution: to help the individual to help himself.

IV. The United Nations World Conference in Bucharest on the Population Explosion.

We in North America live in a world of privilege. And we are going to have to share this world with about three to four billion more people, of whom at least two-thirds will have an annual income of less than $250 a year. We are going to have to recognize as an inevitable prime fact that people are going to demand, as their right, minimum standards of human dignity, human rights, and common decency.

It is evident that in view of the greater and greater scarcity of food, housing, medical care, and education for the present population, it will be catastrophic, even terminal for mankind, if our accelerated population growth continues.

Here again, the Essene Way of Biogenic Living, as described in *The Tender Touch,* offers the solution to the incredible chaos in the field of sex. Through biogenic sexual fulfillment supplementing the uncontrolled biological urges of the emotionally immature irresponsible masses, the fatal population growth (depicted dramatically in our book, *I Came Back Tomorrow*) could be considerably curtailed. As explained in *The Tender Touch,* biogenic sexual fulfillment of the erogenous zones is not intended to completely replace sexual intercourse, but to reawaken 20th century men and women to the ancient, time-hallowed traditions of the spiritualization of the sexual function, returning it to its rightful place on the path of individual evolution—neither stifled by medieval attitudes of prudery, nor abused by permissiveness leading to venereal disease, unwanted pregnancy, and, possibly, all kinds of highly-contagious viral infections. On a purely practical level, this simple program would be enough to restrain irresponsible and immature procreation, proliferated at present mostly by uncontrollable biological urges and ignorance.

V. The United Nations World Conference on Habitat.

This extremely important World Conference really shocked the world by pointing out the sub-human standard of housing for forty percent of the inhabitants of our planet. In my pioneering book on Biogenics published in Paris in 1928, *La Vie Biogenique,** I set down the basic outlines, requirements and practical realization of a healthy, practical, easy-to-build, ecologically sound, esthetically pleasing, and inexpensive miniature biogenic dwelling (described in detail in the chapter *Biogenic Dwelling* in this book). In my original book about Biogenic Living, I anticipated the present imperative requirements fifty years in advance. Had we followed the principles outlined in my book half a century ago, we would be in far better condition today.

VI. The United Nations World Conference in Mexico City on Women.

The position of women in our increasingly complex and industrialized world, with more and more unemployment, unequal wages, and continuing discrimination, is one of growing difficulty, with ever stronger demands made on them. The prevailing self-exploitation, creating artificial needs, adds even greater stress on women because of other aggravating factors.

In the biogenic life style advocated in *The Chemistry of Youth, The Ecological Health Garden,* and *Father, Give Us Another Chance,* women work alongside men; no tasks are arbitrarily assigned because of outmoded medieval traditions and sexist prejudice. Women are liberated from the meaningless drudgery of usual kitchen work and other unnecessary household tasks; men and women automatically become equal partners, living in creative simplicity and relaxed harmonious living.

The Essene Way of Biogenic Living again goes to the root of the problem instead of trying to patch up a basically self-exploitative,

*not to be confused with a current Swiss publication with the same title which is an adaptation of this book and not the author's original volume in French.

complex, unhealthy life situation with superficial, inefficient solutions. The problems of women cannot be solved by legislating equal sharing in a basically wrong, self-exploitative, unhealthy, stressful way of life. Biogenic Living is woman's greatest friend and her fundamental solution. Because, aside from certain fundamental anatomical differences, both sexes are first and foremost human beings, and according to the Essene philosophy, the human soul has no gender.

VII. The United Nations World Conference in Geneva on Unemployment.

If we examine our technological civilization through the eyes of reason, we must realize that everything has simply become too big. Not only is man no longer the measure of all things—but things cannot even be measured anymore. And in this constantly snowballing increase in size and complexity, man is the one who suffers most. In some countries, excessive centralization has created vulnerability to terrorism and strikes, and requires increasing resources and enormous bureaucracy for management; while in socialist countries, the only defense of the worker is passive underachievement. Both Capitalism and Marxism have original sin: they are both based on the concept that the fundamental needs of man are exclusively material.

Is there a way to avoid such a gloomy, catastrophic future? Well, it is apparent to me that the only solution is a slower, steadier rate of economic growth, decentralization, coupled with a reduction in population. These may assure mankind of an adequate if less luxurious mode of living. People should be given the incentive to return to rural areas from huge urban centers, and be employed in smaller, more decentralized, self-sufficient activities. (I explored these ideas many years ago in my book, *Father, Give Us Another Chance.*) The government merely takes money from the citizens in the form of taxes and hands it back to them in the form of welfare, less the paying of politicians and bureaucrats. The economies of the western world are cracking because too many citizens, including politicians and bureaucrats, are taking out of them in the form of salaries, insurance benefits, and welfare, more than they are putting back in the form of production. In other words, the west is running into bankruptcy.

But then, what is the way out? I strongly feel that through the redirection of technology and the right regional planning, it could be possible for the western world to decentralize and still maintain its high productivity. Such a way of living could be supported by small-scale but sophisticated technologies, like solar, wind and geothermal energies, recycling of wastes, etc. The applications should be adjusted locally, according to local conditions.

Sapienti Sat! The Essene Way of Biogenic Living again presents the sane solution to these seemingly insurmountable problems, a ray of practical, workable light in a very troubled world. Please join us to increase our capacity to spread the light. Become a member of our

International Biogenic Society and lend your books on Biogenic Living to your friends, instead of letting them sleep on your shelves (your books, not your friends).

VIII. The United Nations World Conference on Water. The industrial world's skill at treating water is in battle with its ability to pollute water. In the developing world, however, the problem is dirty water. In one-third to one-half of the human settlements of the world, the water is filthy, and one-third of the human race suffers from intestinal diseases. In the western world, diseases such as cholera, typhoid and dysentery are almost forgotten; but for one-third of the human race they are a fact of life, and if you would ask me what would do most, not only to restore dignity to human lives, but which in addition would enable children to survive, I would say clean water in every primitive country.

By clean water, I mean pure, fresh, running water from unpolluted sources, not clean through the use of harmful chemicals, which is the scourge of the civilized countries. Much of our well and faucet water contains high concentrations of nitrite, nitrate, fluoride, chlorine, chlorides, chemical salts, lead, mercury, carbonates of sodium, sulphates, and an endless number of contaminants and chemicals entering daily and continuously our waterways. Chronic poisoning from arsenic may lead to carcinogenous disorders from contaminated drinking water from hundreds of rivers into which we are throwing cumulatively polluted waste, and these are the sources of our local drinking water systems. Industrial and public demands for water continuously grows as our industrial expansion and population is growing, and parallel with these our pollution also grows in accelerated rhythms. Each year, over a thousand new chemical pollutants are developed, and an increasing number of them find their way into our public drinking water.

Here again, Biogenic Living gives us the solution in the form of a small, simple home water distiller, and reduction of necessary use of all water to the minimum. For example, we could reintroduce to western civilization the ancient Sumerian Bath, efficient, meaningful, delightful, and—because of the shallow indentation—extremely frugal in its use of water. Also we recommend the Biogenic Dew Bath for personal hygiene (see *The Tender Touch*) and Biogenic Nutrition based on tender, fresh, juicy sprouts, greens, etc., which make practically negligible the amount of drinking water desired. These practices might well become life savers in a world of less and less usable water and worldwide water pollution.

IX. United Nations World Conference in Nairobi on the Problem of Desertification (continuous growth of deserts and diminution of fertile land).

The world has four billion people [1977], and its population is expected by some experts to double in 25 to 30 years. About fourteen percent of these people live on arid or semi-arid land. According to United Nations estimates, 78 million live on lands already almost

91

useless because of erosion, dune formation, vegetation change, and salt encrustation.

Erosion, deforestation, and, in mismanaged irrigation systems, a buildup of salts in the soil mark the transformation of usable land into desert. Eventually, droughts may trigger the collapse of a vulnerable food production system, resulting in famine.

But we do not have to go into details here. The main point regarding the intelligent use of our precious forest and green belt areas is that the Essene Way of Biogenic Living gives us the practical methods and techniques by which we can maintain and develop these natural resources so vital to our survival. Whether one is the owner of a small lot in the country or an apartment dweller in the city, the Essene Way of Biogenic Living can, among many other things, show us how to improve arid or infertile soil into highly productive biological mini-earth units (see *The Ecological Health Garden, the Book of Survival*). We must not assume as a matter of course that fresh food, in season, locally grown, is an ideal impossible for most people to attain. That assumption is just an excuse to continue to eat the wrong foods. The Essene Way of Biogenic Living provides a method for anyone, regardless of age, profession, or material means, to grow fresh, biogenic food in season, no matter how limited the space available.

X. Planned United Nations World Conference on Energy.

We in North America are wasting at least half of the energy we purchase. Only 6% of each gallon of gas consumed in congested urban driving is used for actual forward motion. Buildings leak like sieves; we probably get 15% to 20% efficiency from our heating systems, and the rest goes out through the roof.

The accumulation of profit-hungry industrial production is wasting and swallowing up the dwindling reserves of our natural resources in general, and of every person in particular. Unless we adapt the Essene Economy of Voluntary Creative Simplicity, and the utilization of replaceable sources of energy, such as sun and wind, we will very soon (much sooner than we think) become bankrupt in all these resources, and civilized life will come to an inglorious end on this planet.

The Essene Way of Biogenic Living at the end of the twentieth century again makes possible (1) the minimization of needed energy, (2) the utilization of replaceable natural energy sources such as sun, water, organic substances, etc., and (3) the restoration of our land to a balanced, natural ecology, providing the only way for homo sapiens to continue to exist on our planet. Here again, the Essene Way of Biogenic Living has the solution.

Conclusions.

The success and increasingly wider acceptance of our Essene Way of Biogenic Living consists in the all-important fact that it offers *practicable, workable, immediate solutions* to all our most urgent, vital problems of mankind. It is an all-sided, complete, *omnilateral* program of living which can be put into practice right here and now, in increasing measures, by anyone, regardless of age, experience, material means or geographical location.

Please join us in these endeavors, which are made increasingly more effective and possible by *your membership* and efficient use of *our literature* to carry this mission all over the world, before it is too late. And it is much later than you think. Let us not be like the metaphysician in the allegory of Buddha, who, instead of removing a poisoned arrow from his side, begins to philosophize about the origin and esoteric meaning of his wound, abruptly dying in the middle of his meditations. Human suffering is the poisoned arrow, according to Buddha. Join us in helping to eliminate human suffering—insuring not only our survival on our planet, but the survival of future generations as well. Let us unite all the forces of Life against the forces of death.

For Further Reading:
Cosmos, Man and Society
Father, Give Us Another Chance
The Chemistry of Youth
The Greatness in the Smallness
The Tender Touch: Biogenic Fulfillment
The Ecological Health Garden, the Book of Survival

BIOGENIC NUTRITION AND BIOGENIC GARDENING

Man is a microcosm in the macrocosm,
Living in a field of permanently varying forces.
His health is harmony with the surrounding
cosmic and natural forces—
His disease, physical or mental,
is disharmony with them.

According to the sum total of our contemporary biochemistry, we have a definite requirement for proteins, fats, carbohydrates, minerals, vitamins, etc. Supposedly, if we go below these nutritional levels, we create a state of malnutrition. When we distilled our experiences with the test groups and control groups over a few decades at Rancho La Puerta, however, we found that in spite of providing carefully and thoroughly all these requirements, in the case of serious ailments, results were statistically not satisfactory.

In view that *contra facta nihil valent argumenta*—against the facts, arguments have no value—I had to conclude that there are, to express it in the language of Shakespeare, many things in heaven and earth which are not only not dreamt of, but which our modern analytical science ignores completely. These are the very things which the ancient Essenes, not through the use of laboratories, but through intuition, knew very well.

I read and read again these words of the Essene Gospel of Peace:

Prepare and eat all fruits of trees, and all grasses of the fields, and all milk of beasts good for eating. For all these are fed and ripened by the fire of life; all are the gift of the angels of our Earthly Mother.

The living angels of the living God serve only living men. For God is the God of the living, and not the God of the dead.

So eat always from the table of God: the fruits of the trees, the grain and grasses of the field, the milk of beasts, and the honey of bees.

For I tell you truly, the God of the living is richer than all the rich of the earth, and his abundant table is richer than the richest table of feasting of all the rich upon the earth. Eat, therefore, all your life at the table of our Earthly Mother, and you will never see want. And when you eat at her table, eat all things even as they are found on the table of the Earthly Mother. Cook not, neither mix all things one with another. And you will never see disease, for such finds favor in the eyes of the Lord.

Then your days will be long upon the earth, for this is pleasing in the eyes of the Lord. Eat always when the table of God is served before you, and eat always of that which you find upon the table of God. For I tell you truly, God knows well what your body needs, and when it needs. For the power of God's angels enters into you with the living food which the Lord gives you from his royal table.

For I tell you truly, the body of the Sons of Man is turned into a temple, and their inwards into an altar, if they do the commandments of God. Wherefore, put naught upon the altar of the Lord when your spirit is vexed, neither think upon any one with anger in the temple of God. And enter only into the Lord's sanctuary when you feel in yourselves the call of his angels, for all that you eat in sorrow, or in anger, or without desire, becomes a poison in your body.

Rejoice, therefore, always with God's angels at their royal table, for this is pleasing to the heart of the Lord. And your life will be long upon the earth, for the most precious of God's servants will serve you all your days: the angel of Joy.

And I also remembered the statements of the Plinius manuscript, describing that

> *". . . they ate only fresh fruits and vegetables, seeds, grains, nuts, legumes, germinated seeds and grains, and tender, small, 'baby' greens, taken fresh from the gardens and orchards right before their meals. . ."*

Then a deep realization suddenly filled me with inner evidence, supported by the practical results we achieved. The Essenes knew, speaking in our contemporary scientific language, that there is something incomparably more important than the stereotyped categorization of foods. They were called healers, or *therapeutae,* by their contemporaries, such as Josephus, Philo, Plinius, etc., and they knew that in order to achieve *optimal* therapeutic results (as they always did), foods must be eaten in their *natural* state, which means: *uncooked, unchanged, whole and fresh from the vegetable garden and orchard, and in small quantities.*

As the Great Experiment* unfolded, we achieved not only the cure of seemingly incurable diseases, but we witnessed the reversal of a number of degenerative diseases and the appearance of inner biological resistance, and all this with a diet below the officially established calorie and protein

---

*See *Search for the Ageless, Volume Two: the Great Experiment,* by Edmond Bordeaux Szekely, available from the International Biogenic Society.

requirements. We invariably found that less food heals faster, and that thirty or forty grams of pure protein, provided it comes from uncooked and unadulterated foods, is as efficient as sixty or eighty grams. It seems that in the Essene nutrition there is a tremendous inner biochemical economy, without waste, providing more nutrients from less. It also seems that we have in the human organism about a thousand enzymes, the correlative functions of which are only little known, of which the majority is destroyed by heating and processing. In view that each year we are discovering new enzymes and enzyme-like biochemical substances, we also have to consider the yet unknown and undiscovered factors which seem to be present in natural, uncooked and unprocessed foods, and which probably perform as vital functions in our metabolism and biochemistry as the already discovered ones. It seemed to me that we were only on the threshold of the great biochemical secrets of life, which the Essenes already knew thousands of years ago.

NEW SCIENTIFIC TERMINOLOGY BASED ON BIOGENIC ACTION

As a first step, I felt I must break away completely from orthodox terminology and create a wholly new scientific term for the mysterious activity of those primordial, natural substances which the Essenes called "living" foods. After careful consideration, I coined the biochemical term of *biogenic* (in Greek, life-generating) foods, in view that these foods, such as seeds, whole grains, nuts, and legumes, have the biochemical capacity, when germinated, to mobilize their dormant life forces and thus virtualize their potentialities to create and generate new life. It became increasingly evident that the classic proteincentric classification of foods, derived from their content of calories, protein, starch, fats, and carbohydrates, must be replaced with a new and revolutionary method of classification, centered around the different degrees of life-generating and cell-renewal capacities of different foods, the creative action of which became so impressively apparent to us during the Great Experiment, even in theoretically incurable cases, again and again through a third of a century, through thousands of our medical histories.

I also had to find a name to indicate those natural, unprocessed foods, such as uncooked fresh fruits and vegetables which, though unable to generate a new, living organism (as the biogenic seeds were able to do), still were capable of sustaining perfectly the already existing life forces in the human organism. I called these life-sustaining substances *bioactive* foods. Biogenic and bioactive foods are able to *synthesize entirely new* compounds and substances which can perform *superior* biogenical and biological functions, destroying biostatic and biocidic substances, microbes and faulty digestive processes. They strengthen the oxygen transport, cell respiration and biological resistance, accelerate cell renewal and through *more efficient* metabolic action stimulate the natural self-healing process (according to Plinius, *vis medicatrix naturae*), strengthening it decisively even in cases of carcinoma. All of this we witnessed in great astonishment, again and again through a third of a century of the Great Experiment.

With our biogenic and bioactive foods, we not only avoided the destruction of enzymes, the deterioration of the quality of certain amino acids and protein foods, the creation of toxic substances of fats through heat, the destruction of vitamins through processing, the addition and removal of substances to and from natural foods, but we also observed a very interesting phenomenon: these biogenic and bioactive foods were digested without increase of leukocytes in the stomach (which always occurs with foods denatured by heat and processing), leaving the leukocytes free in the blood-stream for more efficient defense.

After creating these two new names—biogenic, for life-generating, and bioactive, for life-sustaining foods—I had to find a third term for foods which are not life-generating nor life-sustaining, but which simply slow down the life processes in the organism, accelerating the process of aging. Under this term would be included cooked foods and foods which were not fresh, etc. I gave to this category the term *biostatic* foods.

Finally, for food which contains harmful substances, such as chemicals, additives, adulterants, preservatives, etc., and which have been refined and processed, I gave the name of *biocidic,* or life-destroying foods.

The great Greek philosopher, Protogoras, said that "Man is the measure of all things." In this spirit, it seemed to me that these four new terms, clarifying the function of food in the process of life-generating, life-sustaining, life-slowing, and life-destroying, were more adequate, scientific and practical than the classic four categories of protein, fat, starch, and carbohydrates, which denote mainly the chemical composition of foods rather than their vital function in the body.

While this orthodox classification of food categories was based on their chemical composition, the Essene, or biogenic, nutrition emphasized the central, vital principle: *Foods must be living, and there shall not be a time lapse between the still-living plant organism and its ingestion in still-living condition into the human organism.* This is why, according to the Plinius manuscript, the Essenes *ate directly the still-growing* sprouts, baby greens, vegetables, and fruits, in all their life-generating and life-sustaining potential. There was no storing, no processing, no preserving, no canning, and no freezing. *These foods went directly and instantaneously from the soil or tree to the mouth.* And it was this simple and amazing method which, through a third of a century of our Great Experiment with more than 123,000 people at Rancho La Puerta, created our amazing statistics of recovery of theoretically incurable cases (about 17% of the total participants and test groups).

THE TEN BASIC ESSENTIALS OF A PERFECT DIET

1. You shall eliminate from your diet any food from which vital nutrients have been removed, such as white flour, white sugar, and all those foods in which these devitalized substances are hidden in disguised forms, as they are all *biocidic* (a list of them might go into the thousands.

2. Artificial processing, factorizing, in a word, any process which alters the natural state of a food, destroys vital nutrients and creates *biocidic* foods.

3. Excessive (commercial) storage, such as canning, preserving, freezing, artificial ripening, etc., causes depletion or complete destruction of vitamins, enzymes, plant hormones, etc., and creates *biocidic* foods.

4. Artificial, synthetic additives, such as chemical preservatives, anti-oxidants, humectants, emulsifiers, colorings,

etc., are extremely dangerous and may even be carcinogenic. All these foods are *biocidic* and pathogenic; there is no such thing as a "safe" or "harmless" quantity of these chemical substances. And do not expect the label to reveal the whole truth about what artificial substances and chemical additives may be contained inside a can, package or container. Every food which is commercially processed in any way may be considered to contain additives of some kind.

5. Artificial substitutes of natural foods are not only *biostatic,* but may be *biocidic.*

6. Long storage in the home will also seriously deplete the nutritive value of foods, even those which may originally have been of high quality.

7. Always choose fresh, raw fruits and vegetables, and avoid canned or prepared foods, even those which may come from a "health store."

8. Your diet shall contain fresh, organic fruits and vegetables, whole grains, seeds, beans, nuts, yoghurt, clabbered milk and cottage cheese, made at home from fresh, raw milk, and fresh eggs from healthy, well-nourished chickens who have plenty of fresh air and exercise. Fresh, raw milk should come from healthy, well-nourished goats or cows.

9. The two most important factors in the diet should consist of, (1) embryonic vegetable substances, or *Biogenic Foods,* and (2) of fresh, unprocessed, whole bionutrients, or *Bioactive Foods.* Cooked, stale, unfresh foods, called *Biostatic Foods,* should be avoided as much as possible, and under no condition should processed, chemicalized, denatured, or flesh foods, called *Biocidic Foods,* ever be eaten.

10. Although we have less control over the environment than our diet, we should still avoid as much as possible polluted air, water, land, industrial by-products, contaminated substances, and dangerous radiations.

SEVEN ADVANTAGES OF SIMPLE, BASIC, NATURAL WHOLE FOODS

Simple, basic, natural, whole foods, such as seeds, whole grains, nuts, beans, etc., are our salvation in this increasingly superchemicalized world. They have tremendous advantages:

First: They did not go through the endless steps of chemicalization, denaturization, factorization, and contamination, each step of which makes foods less and less fit for human consumption.

Second: Unlike concentrated, refined carbohydrates, they are not quickly converted into sugar in the biochemistry of the organism; they are digested slowly.

Third: They contain more bulk, therefore, are more satisfying. They satisfy hunger better and prevent overeating and overweight.

Fourth: They release their energy gradually, thereby avoiding extreme highs and lows in the blood-sugar level.

Fifth: Due to their bulk and moisture-absorbing qualities, they insure regular peristaltic movements of the colon, preventing constipation and its multiple harmful effects.

Sixth: They supply a great variety of essential amino acids, unsaturated fatty acids, minerals, vitamins, trace minerals, plant hormones, and plant enzymes.

Seventh: They are *biogenic,* the most important factor of all. They are viable, with the ability and potentiality to mobilize their dormant life forces and *generate life.*

CELLS, ENVIRONMENTAL FLUIDS, DEFICIENCIES, DISEASES, AGING, ILLNESS

In the organism, the functions of growth and repair are continuously taking place. Therefore, the cells and tissues must bathe at all times in fluids (forming the natural environment of our cells) which contain all the essential nutrients. In the absence of this beneficial internal environment, deficiencies will inevitably develop. Deficiencies may cause acute symptoms like influenza, constipation, gastric troubles, headaches, etc., or chronic ailments, such as cancer, arthritis, cardiovascular ailments, diabetes, etc. If our environmental fluids adequately nourish the cells, these diseases can be avoided and prevented, and the totality of their cumulative effects, accelerating the process of aging, can be conclusively slowed down. For instance, wrinkling of the skin of the aged is due to the shrinking of the collagen fibers, concomitant symptoms of the process of aging. An optimal well-balanced diet, and mineral and vitamin supplementation, containing the right balance of all essential nutrients in natural, easily-assimilable form, will greatly assist the slowing-down of the aging process.

OUR SELF-REGENERATING POWER

The Romans called it *vis medicatrix naturae.* The Greeks called it, "Healing yourself."

Through biogenic and bioactive nutrition, natural and simple living, following the path of moderation in all things, we will surely reach what we call *The Essene Way.* Then we will develop and use life-generating and self-healing powers, incomparably greater than those of any physician. This regenerative power will produce powerful antibodies against infections, will knit our fractured bones, and heal our wounds. Our bloodstream will penetrate through our whole organism and perform seemingly miraculous repairs.

PRACTICAL ADVANTAGES OF GERMINATING AND SPROUTING

Sprouts are the most economical and abundant of all foods. One pound of beans will produce about eight pounds of sprouts. Just one flat teaspoon of alfalfa seeds will produce a generous eight ounces of sprouts. They are extremely easy to grow, as we will describe shortly. The usual problems which affect most crops, such as storms, blight, drought, bugs, and chemical spray never hinder sprouts. There is no waste, no physical exertion or need for irrigation schemes.

Sprouts can be germinated from any whole unhulled seed or bean, such as alfalfa, mung beans, soya beans, peas, sesame seeds, wheat, oats, lentils, rye, corn, millet, etc. etc.

MULTILATERAL ADVANTAGES OF GERMINATES AND SPROUTS
AS COMPARED TO USUAL GARDENING

—Independence from soil conditions, composting or fertilizing techniques, insect problems, blight, weeds, sprays, weather or climatic conditions, seasons of the year.

—Simplicity of harvesting: no digging, cutting, dirty hands, or muddy feet.

—Speed of harvesting: from sprout container to salad bowl in a few seconds.

—Inexpensive: seeds, grains and beans quadruple or sextuple their volume in sprouting.

—No soil required, nor hydroponics.

—Requires practically no equipment, only a few quart jars.

—Anyone can learn to sprout. Age is no factor, nor is physical condition.

—Care of sprouts takes only a few minutes, morning and evening.

—Gives a harvest every few days, about an average of 100 crops a year.

—Occupies very little space. Can be done indoors or outdoors, in city or country.

Conclusion: Especially in those climates with long, cold winters, sprouts are the simplest, easiest, most practical (and delicious) inexpensive solution to supply the whole family with fresh, organically-grown, vitamin-, mineral-, enzyme-, and protein-rich *biogenic* food.

FACTS AND FINDINGS OF EXPERIMENTAL RESEARCH FROM SEVEN UNIVERSITIES

—Dr. Ralph Bogart, *Kansas Agricultural Experimental Station,* sprouted oats and found in a quantity of 40 grams, 15 mg. of Vitamin C, more than in the corresponding amount of fresh blueberries, blackberries, or honeydew melon.

—Dr. Berry Mack, *University of Pennsylvania,* found that his sprouted soya beans by the end of 72 hours had a 553% increase in Vitamin C.

—Dr. C. Bailey, *University of Minnesota,* found only negligible amounts of Vitamin C in wheat, but after a few days of sprouting, he found a 600% increase.

—Dr. Andrea at *McGill University,* found 30 mg. of Vitamin C per 110 grams of sprouted dry peas, favorably comparable to orange juice.

—Dr. Beeskow, *Michigan Agricultural Experimental Station,* found the maximum of Vitamin C in sprouts after 50 hours of sprouting.

—Dr. Paul Burkholder, *Yale University,* found the Vitamin B2 content of sprouted oats increased by 1300%, and when the little green leaves appeared on the sprouts, the amount increased to over 2000%. He also found the following approximate increases in: Pyridoxin (B6): 500%, Pantothenic Acid: 200%, Folic Acid: 600%, Biotin: 50%, Inositol: 100%, and Nicotinic Acid: 500%.

—Dr. Francis M. Pottenger, Jr., M.D., from California, found sprouted legumes and beans to contain first quality, complete proteins.

—Dr. Clive McCay, *Cornell University*, wrote a series of articles recommending a "kitchen garden" of sprouts in every home to produce fresh sprouts through the year.

Based on my own experience at Rancho La Puerta, I have simplified the sprouting process even further, and modified it somewhat so that it may be done by virtually anyone, anywhere, under almost any conditions.

What you will need: 4 or 5 wide-mouth quart jars, several four-inch-square pieces of ordinary cheesecloth, and several strong rubber bands.

First step: soak one tablespoon of viable, organically-grown alfalfa seeds in a quart jar, with enough water to cover the seeds.

Next morning: place a piece of cheesecloth over the top of the quart jar and fasten with a rubber band. Rinse the seeds very well by running tap water into the jar, then upend it and let the water run out through the cheesecloth. Repeat this procedure again, and perhaps once more on this first morning, to get rid of all the phytates in the first soaking water. (Phytates are nature's insecticide, provided by her to protect the seed against microorganisms in the soil during the delicate germination process. Since these seeds are not in the soil, the phytates are unnecessary and not a good idea to ingest, as they interfere with certain biological functions in the organism.) When the water runs clear and there is no odor, it is probable that the phytates have been washed away.

Now that the seeds are well-rinsed, find a place with medium temperature, not too hot nor too cold, to keep the sprouting jars. As the jar should be in a *diagonal position* in order for the seeds to sprout (seeds should be neither dry nor drowned), and, as a few drops of excess water will always run out after rinsing, a corner of the bathtub is an excellent place (don't forget to remove the jars before you take a bath!). Actually, if a tray is put under the jars to catch any drops of water, the jars may be put in almost any part of the house or apartment where the temperature is not too cold or hot. The easiest way to keep the jars diagonal is to put them in a dish drainer, used for drying dishes and usually found in every kitchen. The bars of the drainer hold the jar in a diagonal

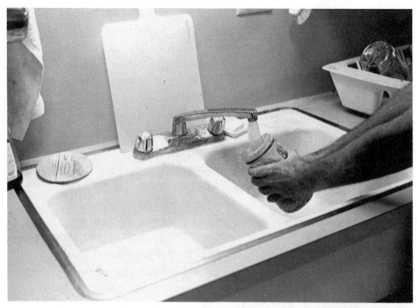

position, and a large one can accommodate as many as four quart jars. In addition to the *diagonal position,* the sprouting seeds must have *darkness,* and plenty of *air.* Therefore, if the room you have chosen is not dark, simply put a towel over the dish drainer which you can remove when you rinse the seeds. Why do the seeds need to be in the dark? Because you are duplicating the natural growth of the seeds in the soil, where they sprout *before* bursting forth into the air and sunlight. Once they do, they are no longer sprouts, but baby green plants. The maximum amount of biogenic energy is contained in the sprout before it contacts the light of day. But sprouting seeds always need air; therefore, be sure the towel does not cover the opening of the jar, which should be covered with cheesecloth only (and just one layer of that).

That night: repeat the rinsing procedure. Apart from the very first time, two rinsings are enough. Incidentally, if your tap water is chlorinated, or of questionable purity, give the final rinsing with a little distilled or spring water.

Also that night: start soaking another tablespoon of alfalfa seeds in a second jar (remember that one tablespoon of dry seeds will make more than a pint of sprouts).

Note: It will be a good idea to date the jars. The simplest label is a bit of masking tape, easy to write on.

The second morning: repeat the procedure of the morning before, this time with two jars. When you are done, there will be two jars in diagonal position in the dish drainer.

This entire procedure is repeated, with morning and evening rinsings, until there are four jars, side by side, in the dish drainer. On the fifth day, the alfalfa sprouts you prepared the first day are ready to harvest. On the morning of the fifth day, give the ready alfalfa sprouts an extra-good rinsing with pure water, and let them drain in a collander before putting them in the refrigerator, in a container which is exposed to air but covered loosely with plastic to avoid drying out.

Eat these alfalfa sprouts on the day they are ready! It is extremely important to *always consume the sprouts on the day they are harvested*—this is the meaning and purpose of *biogenic nutrition,* the significance of the term *life-generating.*

This is why we work with four jars, instead of only one. Sprouting seeds in only one jar is easier, but then you will have fresh sprouts only once every five days—or, what is worse, you may be tempted to make a large amount and then keep it in the refrigerator for five days. It is far better to make a small amount (with a little experimentation you will know how much you can eat in a day and adjust the amount of dry seed accordingly) and eat it fresh every day, than to make a large amount and store it. Biogenic food can become biostatic food if it loses its freshness. (This is why sprouts found in supermarkets are so often in pathetic condition and completely inedible.)

All of this is much easier to do than to write about. Rinsing is very simple, as the water simply flows into the jar, then out again when you turn the jar upside down (the seeds do not flow out with the water, as they are held back by the cheesecloth). The dish drainer makes it easy to keep the jars in a diagonal position. Once the rhythm is attained, the whole routine takes but a few minutes morning and evening, and the rewards are astronomical in relation to the effort made. I want to add this important caution: do not make the sprouting procedure complicated! There is nothing complicated about it, and it should become as natural and second-nature as brushing your teeth.

One of the fallacies that exists about sprouting is that unless conditions are perfect in regard to air flow, humidity, ventilation, sterilization, etc., the seeds will not sprout. I want to emphasize that there is only *one* reason why seeds will not sprout, if these simple instructions are followed, and that is if the seeds themselves are not viable, or fresh. If your seeds do not sprout, take them back to the store and find another source. Viable seeds are so eager to sprout, it often happens that one or two will fall down behind the dish drainer, and in a week or so you suddenly find an alfalfa plant growing up!

I am also aware that there are many types of sprouting equipment available, some of the latest ones very sophisticated (and expensive). The reason I have chosen to describe the method using quart jars, cheesecloth, and rubber bands, is

not because this is the only way to sprout seeds, but because it is the simplest and most inexpensive way.

Nothing is so rewarding, so tremendously beneficial in relation to the small amount of effort required, as the sprouting of alfalfa seeds. It is a miracle biogenic food, growing to full potency in only four days, requiring only a simple rinse morning and night. And the same method can be used with other seeds and legumes (with slight variations in soaking and sprouting time) such as wheat, rye, lentils, mung beans, soya beans, and many more. However, alfalfa sprouts are by far the most popular, both for their delicious taste as well as their eagerness to sprout.

PANORAMA OF THE CORNUCOPIA OF BIOACTIVE (LIFE-SUSTAINING) FOODS OF OPULENT MOTHER EARTH

Thirty-four fruits: Apple — Pear — Peach — Apricot — Plum — Prune — Nectarine — Orange — Lemon — Lime — Grapefruit — Mango — Papaya — Persimmon — Pineapple — Cherimoya — Guava — Jujube — Sapodilla — Sapote — Strawberry — Raspberry — Huckleberry — Blackberry — Blueberry — Currants, red and black — Gooseberry — Grape — Cherry — Pomegranate — Watermelon — Canteloupe — Honeydew Melon — Banana — and many more.

Twenty-one raw vegetables: Tomato — Cucumber — Carrot — Cabbage — Beet Greens — Kohlrabi — Jerusalem Artichoke — Lettuce — Cauliflower — Celery — Watercress — Green Pepper — Mustard — Kale — Swiss Chard Greens — Dandelion Leaf — Green Onion — Chives — Garlic — Dill — Parsley — and many more.

THE TEN MOST IMPORTANT BIOACTIVE FRUITS OF THE ANCIENT ESSENES

Olives — Almonds — Pistachio Nuts — Pomegranates — Figs — Grapes — Dates — Small Yellow Apples — Apricots — Carob.

THE POTENTIALLY BIOGENIC FOODS
Seeds — Grains — Nuts — Beans

Seeds: Sunflower — Sesame — Pumpkin — Alfalfa — Chia — Mung
Grains: Wheat — Rye — Triticale — Rice — Corn — Millet — Oats — Barley — Buckwheat
Nuts: Almond — Walnut — Pecan — Hazel Nut (Filbert) — Cashew — Brazil — Pignolia (Pine Nut)
Beans: Soya — Lentil — Peanut — Peas — Kidney — Blackeye

BIOACTIVE BABY GREENS: THE "INSTANT" INDOOR VEGETABLE GARDEN

In my book, *The Ecological Health Garden, the Book of Survival,* I discuss the subject of gardening extensively, and I recommend the study of this book to anyone who is starting an outdoor garden. Here, however, I am mainly concerned with the best method of supplying in as short a time as possible a constant, ample supply of bioactive green leaves for the daily diet, greens free from pesticides or chemical fertilizers—*greens freshly picked moments before eating.*

First of all, the containers for the baby greens should be simple, light, and portable. Ornamental planters are too heavy and ornate, and hanging containers are impractical. Shallow wooden boxes are fine, but not everyone will be able to find them or construct them. The best thing is an ordinary shallow plastic bucket, not more than 4½ inches deep, with a wide (ten inch diameter) opening, available at any hardware store. Plastic five-quart paint buckets are just about perfect for our purpose. They are so light that even filled with earth they are easy to move with their handle from place to place. They are so inexpensive that many may be purchased at once, making possible continuous planting. If you are always careful not to use too much water, just enough to keep the soil moist, you do not even need drainage holes. And with no drainage holes, the buckets can be placed anywhere in your home without damaging rugs, furniture, etc.

What to put into the bucket? That depends on where you live. If you have access to good rich soil, uncontaminated by pesticides and free from impurities, then by all means fill your bucket from an outdoor source. But otherwise, use an organic potting soil mixture available from any nursery, making sure it is free from chemicals. Due to the current popular interest in house plants, bags of potting soil are available these days even in supermarkets.

Where to put the buckets? That also depends on where you live and how much room you have. If there is room to spare, a very simple construction of shelves can be made by placing 1x4 inch boards over concrete blocks. This simple shelf construction will hold a great number of buckets and can easily be dismantled and put up again. If there is no room for the shelves, then the buckets can simply be kept on window sills or anywhere there is light.

Once the buckets are filled with soil and placed where there is light, at least part of the day, and you have on hand

a small watering can (very small, for the ideal is always just to keep the soil moist—never, never drown your baby greens, particularly if you have no drainage hole in the bottom of the bucket), you are ready to start your indoor garden. And since the object is to have a flourishing garden ready for harvesting in a matter of days and not weeks, here is a list of those baby greens which will grow almost instantly:

Garlic Greens. While many people cannot eat garlic, everyone enjoys the tender green leaves of the baby garlic plant, with their delicate flavor. Buy only the best quality garlic bulbs for planting, preferably large, white, and hard to the touch. Separate the bulb into cloves and plant them in the bucket with the pointed end up (if you plant the clove upside down, it will not grow!), not any deeper than the length of the clove itself, and very close together, approximately an inch apart. In one bucket of ten-inch diameter, you should be able to plant about forty cloves. (Remember that you are going to eat these greens in their biogenic stage, so you do not need to allow for extensive root growth.) In order to have a nice helping of garlic greens daily in your salads and other biogenic and bioactive dishes, it is a good idea to plant two buckets of garlic greens once a month. Depending on the season, the little green shoots will appear in as little as three days, and when the greens are around eight inches tall, snip them off close to the soil, but never pull out the plant. In this way, the green shoots will continue to grow and may be snipped off several times before the plant finally turns brown. (And even then, if you plant the contents of the buckets in your outdoor garden, you may be surprised to see it come to life again, as the root system extends itself and recognizes its natural home, the earth.)

Onion Greens. There are several ways to have green onions almost instantly in your indoor garden. One way is to buy from your local nursery onion sets, or multiplier onions, tiny bulbs which grow almost immediately after planting. (Plant them exactly as you do the garlic cloves, not deep and very close together.) Another way, which is even faster, depending on the season, is to look for ordinary cooking onions in the market which have started to sprout. Even if you can see just a speck of green showing at the top of the onion, you can be sure it will thrive and bloom once it has contact with the soil in your bucket. Depending on the size of the onion, you can put two or three of them in the same bucket (make sure the onion is completely covered with soil, as these larger ones will need more room for their roots) and you will be astonished when you see the seemingly never-ending supply of green onion shoots they will produce.

Lentil Greens. Few people realize the biogenic potential of lentils. One of the most ancient foods of man, described not only in the Bible but in more ancient literature as well, lentils, when planted, provide delicious, tender greens for salads. And nothing could be easier to grow!

First, soak one-third of a cup of ordinary brown lentils in about a pint of tepid water overnight. In the morning, rinse the lentils well and set them to sprout exactly as with the alfalfa seeds, described previously. Rinse them morning and evening, just as you do with the alfalfa sprouts, and in about two days the lentil sprouts will be as long as your thumbnail. Fill one of your shallow plastic buckets with soil and spread the lentil sprouts over the top, like a carpet. Keep the sprouts moist until the roots have found their way into the soil, set the bucket in a place where there is plenty of light (not necessarily direct sunlight), and in about five days you will be amazed to see leafy green shoots as tall as four inches! Once you have snipped them off, the leafy parts usually will not grow again, so it is a good idea to have one portion of lentils sprouting while another is growing. Snip off the lentil greens only when you are ready to eat them, so the full biogenic potential will be realized in the organism.

A MINIATURE INDOOR HERB GARDEN

If you are interested in growing herbs extensively indoors, I suggest the reading of my book *The Chemistry of Youth,* in which the subject is described in detail. The role of herbs in nutrition is covered in my book *The Book of Herbs.*

THE EDUCATIONAL, HEALTH, AND PSYCHOLOGICAL VALUES OF INDOOR GARDENING FOR THE YOUNG AND OLD

There can be no better way to teach a child about the miracle of nature, than through the indoor garden. Its value is obvious for the child who lives in an apartment in the city; but even for the country child, the indoor garden provides a ringside seat in the magical theatre of nature, a spectacle which can be enjoyed at any time of the day, no matter what the weather is outside.

Why is the indoor garden so much more intriguing and fascinating to a child than the outdoor garden? The main reason is the time factor. To a child, a month is an incredibly long time, and three months is an eternity. It is often difficult for a child to associate the tiny seed that was planted in May with the tall plants and vines that mature in August. In the indoor garden, however, garlic cloves will push up their green shoots in a matter of two days, and tiny onion sets will do the same. What a marvelous way to impart the truth of the eternal cycle of life to a child, when he sees a mature beet planted in the soil, and a few days later watches the baby green leaves appear!

Sprouting is even more magical. The method of sprouting is so simple (as is all indoor gardening) the child can handle the entire operation himself, and it is an unforgettable thrill to see the sprout and root forming from the tiny seed, reaching lengths of several inches in only four or five days. All children love secrets, and to be a part of the sprouting cycle is to know first hand what happens to the seed deep in the soil before it sends up its green shoots.

The opportunities for education are endless—lessons of life, growth, cooperation, not to mention the obvious invaluable message of good nutrition. A child who grows up with the happy responsibility of taking care of an indoor garden of baby greens and sprouts cannot help but feel profoundly the important role these greens should always play in his nutrition. They become a gift of nature, a magical creation which he helped to bring to life—food which truly lives. Children have good instincts, and these tiny, tasty, living greens and sprouts, grown under their own supervision, will be eaten with relish and enjoyed for a lifetime, with incalculable future health benefits.

For the elderly, the indoor garden can be just as valuable, just as magical. In addition to the economic advantages of the indoor garden, the greens and sprouts provide a rich storehouse of vitamins, minerals, plant hormones and plant enzymes, which simply do not exist in produce from the store, which has lost up to two-thirds of its original vitality by the time it is actually purchased. Also, many older people have trouble digesting roughage, and virtually all of the greens in the supermarket are, to put it kindly, mature. To make these old vegetables palatable, they have to be cooked, and by so doing, most of the vitamins and enzymes are lost. Baby greens, on the other hand, are very easily digested by even the most delicate and feeble digestive system, because they are so tender and young. People who have given up salads because of intestinal troubles find they can eat raw the miniature baby greens just as they come from the soil. As for sprouts, no food is more readily digestible. Even if they are not chewed perfectly, they assimilate very well in the body, and immeasurably improve general nutrition.

Another benefit to the elderly from the indoor garden is the physical one: the small amount of care needed daily to water the garden, perhaps move the planters to and from sun and shade, rinse the sprouts, etc., is just the right kind of exercise to benefit the organism without tiring it. So many elderly people spend their retirement in city apartments, and the indoor garden is a wonderful way of bringing the beauties and joys of nature to them.

Actually, the indoor garden is a good idea for everyone; it is an activity which, while teaching the ageless laws of nature, provides the ultimate in biogenic and bioactive nutrition. But for the young and the old, it is particularly valuable—an activity to bring wisdom and maturity to the child, and youth and vitality to the elderly.

BIOCIDIC FOODS: HOW TO SURVIVE
OUR CHEMICALIZED FOODS AND ENVIRONMENT

After the second war, an accelerated flood of synthetic and toxic additives inundated our markets and supermarket chains, which soon became all-sidedly omnipresent in *all* products which the innocent and ignorant housewives carried home to deteriorate the health of their families. Instead of purity, freshness, and wholesomeness, the new post-war

criteria for desirable food became taste, texture, and shelf life. In geometrical progression ever since, the greediness of the lethal food industry and the all-pervading sophisticated and deceiving promotion of television and radio have become an omnipresent menace of corruption to the public mind and body.

It is mind-staggering to try to conceive that, according to the statistics of our bicentennial year, 550 different synthetic chemicals, a total of a billion pounds a year in over 32,000 products, are conspiring against the innocent, uninformed, and misinformed consumer, making it very improbable that our nation will survive to celebrate its tricentennial year.

We will mention only a few infinitesimally small categories of these synthetic chemicals: preservatives, emulsifiers, moisturizers, dyes, sprays, bleaches, artificial flavors, gases, antioxidants, hydrogenators, deodorizers, buffering agents, alkalizers, disinfectants, acidifiers, extenders, fungicides, insecticides, drying agents, defoliants, thickeners, neutralizers, conditioners, maturers, antifoaming and anticaking agents, artificial sweeteners, fortifiers, hydrolizers, etc. etc.

Whenever food manufacturers remove a natural substance from a food, they always replace it with a synthetic adulterant. Of course, this manipulation disturbs the whole natural biochemical balance in the food. Each time a synthetic is consumed, the biogenic and biological processes of the organism receive a shock to which they are desperately trying to adjust themselves, very often with little success. Each time, a precondition of disease is added to the already disturbed living processes, developed and perpetuated over millions of years. Their continuous, more and more aggressive disturbance proliferates a long line of chronic and degenerative ailments. Even in ordinary simple foods, a great number of synthetic, and often toxic additives are ingested.

In ice cream: coal tar dye, diglycerides, monoglycerides, antibiotics, artificial flavors, carboxymethyl cellulose, artificial colors, etc.

In apple pie: nicotine, lindane, chlordane, methoxychlor, butylated hydroxyanisole, lead arsenate, demeton, parathion, malathion, hexachloride, benzene, sodium-phenylphenate, etc.

In butter: diacetyl, hydrogen peroxide, coal tar dyes, etc.

In oleomargarine: monoisopropyl citrate, diglycerides, isopropyl citrate, monoglycerides, etc.

In pickled vegetables: sodium nitrate, alum, aluminum sulphate.

In fruit juices: saccharine, parathion, dimethyl polysiloxane, benzoic acid, etc.

In breads: coal tar dye, diglycerides, ditertiary buthyl paracresol, ammonium chloride, polyoxyethylene, monoglycerides.

In meats: stilbestrol, dieldrin, aureomycin, methoxychlor, toxaphene, chlordane, heptachlor, benzene hexachloride, etc.

In potatoes: all kinds of pesticides: ethylene dibromide, heptachlor, dieldrin, chlordane, etc.

We could continue on page after page the endless thousands of synthetic and toxic additives, but I think these few samples are enough. *Sapienti sat!*

CONCLUSION

After reading about all the wonderful values of biogenic sprouts and baby greens, you should not draw the false conclusion that you are meant to live exclusively on these two categories of foods. To advocate *exclusively* such a spartan diet would be contrary to the totality of our acquired habits. We should also enjoy the benefits and pleasure of a great variety of wholesome foods.

In addition to the biogenic sprouts and baby greens, your diet should contain fresh, organic fruits and vegetables, whole grains, seeds, beans, nuts, fresh plain yogurt, clabbered milk, unadulterated cottage cheese, and fresh eggs from healthy, well-nourished chickens who are allowed plenty of fresh air and exercise. Fresh, raw milk should come from healthy, well-nourished goats or cows.

In other words, to the hundreds of wholesome bioactive (and even some good biostatic) foods, you should add at each meal a few ounces of sprouts and baby greens. Expressed in mathematical terms, your diet should consist, basically, of 25% biogenic, 50% bioactive, and 25% biostatic foods. This seems to be the most effective way of coming to terms with life in the twentieth century, at the same time attaining and maintaining that shining physical vitality described so vividly in the *Essene Gospel of Peace*.

DRESSINGS FOR VEGETABLE AND FRUIT SALADS

Here are a few ideas to stimulate more ideas on how to make raw fruits and vegetables tastier:

Basic Dressing for Vegetable Salad

Mix well one part lemon juice and two parts fresh, crude, unrefined coldpressed oil (or four parts mashed avocado).

Variations for Vegetable Salads:

Garlic Dressing

Add to basic dressing one clove mashed garlic.

Herb Dressing

Add to basic dressing dried chervil, thyme, basil and fresh herbs such as dill and parsley. Use amounts to taste.

Cheese Dressing

Grate a few spoons of Parmesan or Swiss Cheese into herb dressing.

Egg Dressing

Mash a raw egg yolk or a mashed hard-boiled egg with lemon juice and crude, raw, fresh vegetable oil.

Avocado Dressing

Mix half of mashed avocado with herb dressing.

Chinese Dressing

Two parts *fresh* soy or peanut oil and one part bean juice mixed with two parts of soy sauce (low-sodium type with no added preservatives). Good with bean sprouts.

Basic Fruit Salad Dressing

Fresh orange juice mixed with yogurt (proportion to taste). Use only natural, home-made yogurt.

Variations for Fruit Salads:

Honey Dressing

Add a few spoons of liquid honey and a teaspoon of grated organic citrus rind to the basic fruit salad dressing.

Seed-Nut Dressing

Add a few ounces of grated sunflower seeds, chopped walnuts and ground sesame seeds to honey dressing.

Mint Dressing

Add a few spoons of fresh, chopped mint leaves to honey dressing.

Snack Suggestions:

Sticks—carrots, celery, turnip, fresh pineapple, rutabaga.

Rings—cucumbers, green peppers, pimento, apples.

Wedges—cabbage, lettuce, tomatoes, oranges, tangerines, pears, apples, fresh pineapple.

Flowerettes—cauliflower, broccoli.

Roses—radishes.

Curls—carrots, celery.

Halves—apricots, plums, peaches.

Toothpick Pickups—cubes of natural, low-fat cheese.

All of the above may be combined with the various dressings for fruit and vegetable salads.

HAZEL

For Further Reading:
The Chemistry of Youth
The Book of Living Foods
Biogenic Reducing: The Wonder Week
Treasury of Raw Foods
Scientific Vegetarianism
The Conquest of Death
Modern Dietetics at a Glance

BIOGENIC LIVING

"Fifty million years ago
Our guardian angel, the grass
Arrived to our planet—
To make life possible
And to prepare the earth
For the human race. . ."

THE MIRACLE OF GRASS

In order to understand the principles and purpose of Biogenic Living, we must first understand the importance and significance in all our lives, of that most humble, ubiquitous and universal of all plants—the grass. According to Sir Fred Hoyle, "the emergence of intelligence on Earth was probably due to a combination of several circumstances, among which the most important was the development about fifty million years ago of the plant now called grass. The emergence of this plant caused a drastic reorganization of the whole animal world, due to the peculiarity that grass can be cropped to ground level, in distinction from all other plants. As the grasslands spread over the Earth, those animals that could take advantage of this peculiarity survived and developed. Other animals declined or became extinct. It seems to have been in this major reshuffle that intelligence was able to gain its first footing on our planet."

The climato-meteorological consequences of the increasing destruction of the rain forests of the world are resulting in devastating dry spells in many parts of our planet. When you live in an environment of concrete, metals, plastic, and other artificial substances, losing your contact with the elements of nature, and mainly with their ancestral synthesis, the plant world, your biopsychological condition will gradually deteriorate. When, in addition, you breathe polluted air, and your body has no more contact with green plants, etc., your individual biosphere gradually diminishes and deteriorates. The generally accepted psychoneurotic problems of the city dweller stem from this destruction of the individual biosphere. The process seems to be not only inevitable but insurmountable.

While you are not able to improve the biosphere of the

whole planet, you can definitely ameliorate at least your immediate micro-environment, in your own room, for example. When your vitality inexorably diminishes because of the absence around you of fast-growing, life-generating, air-filtering young plants, you can do something to re-establish your lost symbiosis with vital, young, fast-growing plants and the more natural air created by them in your living area. Remember, you are breathing 12,000 quarts of air daily. It is our most important food.

It is possible that the phylogenetic longing for contact with the vital, green biogenic zone of our planet, imprinted on the DNA of our cells for hundreds and thousands of years, is the reason for the recent popularity of house plants in the homes and apartments of city dwellers. But no nursery-produced house plant can equal the power and biogenic vitality of the young, fast-growing grass in our *Portable Meadow* and *Biogenic Battery*. With very little effort and expense, we can actually create a mini-forest within our own dwelling, perhaps not as ideal a setting as the cathedral-like forests where our distant ancestors lived in perfect symbiosis with the biogenic forces of nature—but the reality is that we live here and now, in the midst of a highly technological era at the latter part of the twentieth century, and we must do our very best with the tools we have. And with these simple tools—the Portable Meadow and the Biogenic Battery—we can create a self-perpetuating biogenic field of vital forces to surround us, and we can enjoy the same phylogenetic symbiosis with the primeval life forces which our ancestors enjoyed for hundreds and thousands of years.

HOW TO MAKE A PORTABLE MEADOW

"Ours is an unswerving 'Custer's Last Stand'
Against the flood of concrete, metals and plastics
And the pollution of air, water, soil and vegetation—
That humankind may live."

Begin with a simple plastic paint bucket from any hardware store, about 5 to 6 inches deep, and about 10-12 inches in diameter. Fill it with good soil. If you have an outdoor source that is free of pesticides and is of good porous consistency, use it. If not, use an organic potting soil from any nursery, large hardware store, or even a supermarket.

Soak one-half cup of whole wheat grains (or most other whole grains—wheat and rye are best) in water of room temperature in an open glass jar overnight. The next morning, put a layer of cheesecloth over the jar opening, fasten with a rubber band, and rinse the wheat thoroughly by letting water from a faucet run into the jar, then turning it upside down and letting the water run out. Repeat this rinsing several times until the water is clear. If the water from your faucet is chlorinated or otherwise impure, let the last rinsing be with pure bottled (distilled or spring) water.

Set the jar with the rinsed wheat grains in a diagonal position (an ordinary dish drainer is excellent for holding it in a diagonal position) in a dark place for 12 hours. The reason for the diagonal position is so the wheat grains may be evenly distributed over the length of the jar. It is the combination of air and evenly-distributed moisture that encourages the grain to sprout. Because air is so important, do not let anything block the cheesecloth-covered opening. If a dark place is unavailable, simply cover the jar lightly with a porous towel.

After 12 hours, rinse the wheat again, and let it sprout for another 12 hours. After a full 24 hours of sprouting, rinse the grains thoroughly, as described above.

Now spread the sprouted wheat grains like a carpet over the top of the soil in the bucket. Wet the grains thoroughly, but do not completely saturate the soil with water, as there is no drain hole in the bottom of the bucket.

On one side of the wheat grain is the beginning root; on the other end will come the sprout, which eventually will become grass. It takes about a day for the little roots to find their way into the soil, and until they do, it will be a good idea to keep the grain-carpet moist and out of direct sunlight. If you work and have to be away all day, cover the bucket with a large plastic bag, poking a hole in the top for air. This will keep the moisture in, but do not forget to remove it after 24 hours, or the grains may start to mold.

As soon as you see the white shoots start to come up, you can place the bucket in a window-sill, or anywhere the grains

will receive light (it does not have to be direct sunlight). Only an occasional moistening now will be needed, as the shoots very quickly turn green, and the growth from now on is amazingly rapid.

In seven days, the young biogenic grass will be ready for those biogenic practices described in this book.

HOW TO MAKE A BIOGENIC BATTERY

The biogenic battery differs from the portable meadow only in size. It will be a good idea, before starting to plant the first biogenic battery, to acquire about two dozen small cup-size containers in which the opening is about the same diameter as the base: these can be yogurt cartons, small cottage cheese cartons, cardboard cup-size containers from a nursery, even glass or plastic wide-mouth jars that held cosmetics or shampoo (but be sure to wash them very well).

Start the grains soaking as for the portable meadow, but of course the amount is greatly reduced. Do not soak more than one flat tablespoon of grains at a time. Soak the grains in the same way, in an open glass jar, or drinking glass, with the opening covered with one small layer of cheesecloth fastened with a rubber band. The next morning, let faucet water run into the jar, then out again (the cheesecloth will prevent the grains from escaping) and once or twice more to be sure they are thoroughly rinsed. Then set the jar or glass in a diagonal position (it is so small, it will fit in your dish drainer right there in your kitchen) for 12 hours, covering the jar with a small piece of paper towel to keep the grains in darkness.

After 12 hours, fill the cup-size container with soil (not quite to the top) and spread the wheat grains (which by now have started to sprout) evenly over the top of the soil. Moisten the grains thoroughly, but be very careful not to add too much water—remember you are dealing with a very tiny amount of soil.

Cover the little container completely with a small plastic bag (you can poke a tiny hole somewhere in it for air), place a piece of paper towel over that, and set it aside for 12 hours. The plastic bag assures that the grains will stay moist while the little root-sprouts are finding their way into the soil, and it also makes it convenient for those who have to work all day and cannot be home to occasionally moisten the grains.

After 12 hours, moisten the grains again and replace the plastic bag. In another 12 hours (24 hours in all using the plastic bag) remove the plastic, and place the little container on a window-sill. Only very occasional moistening will be necessary now as the white shoots will come up very rapidly, turn green, and soon be transformed into tender green leaves.

After seven days, and until the fourteenth day, the biogenic battery will be ready for the biogenic meditation. From the fourteenth until the twenty-first day, the biogenic battery will be ready for the biogenic fulfillment practices.

CONTINUOUS PLANTING OF THE BIOGENIC BATTERY

Obviously, a system of continuous planting is necessary; otherwise, you will be able to take advantage of the multiple uses of the biogenic battery only once a month. A 7-day cycle is best, and once the routine is established, you will find it is extremely easy and becomes almost second-nature.

Before we continue with a description of some of the uses of the Portable Meadow and the Biogenic Battery, there is an anticipated question I want to answer, for those who wonder why they cannot simply go outdoors to their lawn, their flower garden or vegetable patch, and receive the same benefits of the biogenic force field? Why is it necessary to plant whole grains in small buckets and containers when outdoors (if you are lucky enough not to live in the city) there are all kinds of plants, trees and grass growing? The answer lies in the word *biogenic.* When you plant these whole grains, within a short seven days the grass is several inches high—a veritable starburst of explosive, vital, life-generating *biogenic* energy—energy which the fast-growing plant shares with you—energy which surrounds you, flows through you, nourishes you, and revitalizes you. Once the plant reaches its *bioactive* stage, after about three weeks, the plant still has plenty of energy to maintain itself, but not enough to share with you. When it gets older, and reaches its *biostatic,* or aging phase, then it has just enough energy to barely maintain itself. And of course, the *biocidic,* or dying, state follows naturally, as the plant returns to the earth which gave it life, and a new cycle begins. The grass on your front lawn and the vegetables in your garden are most likely in the bioactive stage and have no excess energy to share with you. This is why we recommend, as the first step on the road to Biogenic Living, the planting of the Portable Meadows and Biogenic Batteries, to provide you with a continuous supply of vital, life-generating biogenic energy, from the vast primeval life-stream of our planet, of which we are an inextricable part.

In addition to providing biogenic energy simply by sharing our existence, there are many things we can do with the Portable Meadow and Biogenic Battery to increase our health, vitality, and even our individual evolution. I would like to describe here some of the more simple of these ancient uses, which are particularly important to our survival in this technologically-oriented century, when our air, water and food are so vulnerable to contamination. By the correct use of the Portable Meadow and the Biogenic Battery, we can greatly improve the quality of our air, our sleep, our ability to relax, and even our personal hygiene.

BIOGENIC RELAXATION IN THE MEADOW

I do not need to impress on the reader the vital need for a healthy and efficient method of relaxation in our tense and troubled world. Tranquilizers and sleeping pills are dispensed like candy by physicians who should know better, but even these harmful chemical crutches do not help to alleviate the underlying anxiety which accompanies our steady drift away from our phylogenetic world of green grass and tall trees.

Unlike artificial and harmful methods, this method of biogenic relaxation *works*—because it utilizes the powerful biogenic force field of the Portable Meadow. The silence which surrounds you is the silence of the forest—alive with growth, vitality, and the quiet joy of nature.

The method:

1. Place the Portable Meadow on a table.
2. Bring a comfortable chair to the table.
3. Sit in a comfortable position in the chair for ten minutes, close as possible to the Portable Meadow.

The Biogenic force field emanating from the meadow surrounds you and penetrates your whole body for ten refreshing minutes, as you absorb it. You can enjoy biogenic relaxation in the meadow whenever you feel tense or tired.

BIOGENIC SLEEP IN THE MEADOW

The ancient Essenes knew that sleep, as well as providing the body with the preconditions for biological repair, can be a source of the deepest knowledge. They believed that when the last thoughts before sleep were harmonious ones, the subconscious would be put in contact with the great storehouse of superior cosmic forces, described in greater detail in the chapter *Biogenic Psychology*. But it is often extremely difficult these days for people to achieve a really good night's sleep. Digestion may be working overtime, unsolved problems and anxieties may be fermenting in the mind, and in the city, pollution and absence of growing green plants may deprive the brain of the oxygen it needs for restful sleep.

By utilizing the powerful biogenic force field of the Portable Meadow through the night, the quality of sleep is vastly improved. Not only is the oxygen content of the air increased, but the vital, biogenic energies absorbed contribute to our gradual ability to contact more and more the regenerating flow from the primeval Ocean of Life.

The method:
1. Place the Portable Meadow on a small, 18-inch tall table, as close as possible to the head end of your bed.
2. Just go to sleep at night as usual, making sure you have fresh air.

The biogenic force field will surround you and penetrate into your whole body during the night, while you absorb it.

BIOGENIC BREATHING IN THE MEADOW

Complicated breathing exercises are completely superfluous; it matters not *how* we breathe, but *what* we breathe. Brisk walking in fresh, pure air is the best breathing exercise; complex techniques of breathing performed in a stuffy room in the middle of a polluted city can do only harm to the body. Air is our most important food—we take in more than twelve thousand quarts of it a day. No matter where we live, by adopting this simple method of biogenic breathing in the meadow, we can create a vital, oxygen-rich atmosphere—even while driving in our cars (the Portable Meadow is much more efficient than air conditioning to provide a biogenic atmosphere in the auto, even in the midst of heavy traffic with its choking fumes).

The method:

1. Place the Portable Meadow on a table.
2. Bring a comfortable chair to the table.
3. Sit in a comfortable position in the chair and lean forward toward the table, supporting your elbows. Then inhale and exhale gently, without strain, your breathing directed toward the meadow. Breathe in and out altogether seven times, with short, natural intervals between exhaling and inhaling.

You breathe in the subtle, new-mown-haylike fragrance from the green leaves of grass, with the emanating oxygen, and exhale the carbon dioxide waste from your lungs. This sevenfold biogenic breathing can be enjoyed at any time you need refreshment. (While driving, simply place the Portable Meadow on the seat next to you and forget about it. It will do its biogenic work while you keep your eyes on the road!)

BIOGENIC DEW BATH

The biogenic dew bath is an adaptation of a very ancient technique used in many civilizations of the past. It utilizes the refreshing dew from tender young grass in order to cleanse, invigorate and revitalize the whole body. It is also an ingenious way to thoroughly wash the body using only half a pint of water! That is quite a contrast to the gallons and gallons wasted in a traditional shower or bath. The biogenic dew bath is taken with the Biogenic Battery, not the Portable Meadow.

The method:

1. Undress indoors or outdoors in a comfortable temperature.
2. Dip the grass of the Biogenic Battery (holding the container firmly) into water of room temperature. Be sure not to get the soil wet, only the grass (which should be at least 7-10 days old).
3. Gently and quickly sponge all accessible parts of the body with the wet grass.

4. After your short dew bath, walk around for a few minutes until you are dry.

The fine capillary nerves and veins in your skin will be stimulated and refreshed, transmitting this fresh and invigorating feeling through the whole body, parallel with the absorption of biogenic energy from the force field of the Biogenic Battery. You may enjoy this biogenic dew bath any time you feel the need of refreshing invigoration.

One important thing to remember: the container, seeds and soil used for the Biogenic Battery must be very *clean* and free from chemicals to prevent any skin trouble through contact.

Animals are frequently attracted to the powerful, life-generating energy in the fast-growing grass. A few seconds after this photo was taken, Prince had his nose buried in the seven-day-old Portable Meadow, purring happily.

For Further Reading:
The Ecological Health Garden, the Book of Survival
Cosmos, Man and Society
Father, Give Us Another Chance
The Greatness in the Smallness

BIOGENIC DWELLING

At present, our usual and traditional conventional dwelling has many deficiencies. It is usually unsound ecologically, ruinous to the environment, tremendously wasteful in energy, in building materials, in *space,* in cost, in safety, in healthfulness, and generally lacking in esthetic appeal. It does not function according to the laws of nature—it is not an integral part of it.

These facts have been recognized by many modern architects, and one of the solutions created as a result was the geodesic dome, and its successors. Nevertheless, even these attempts to break away from tradition disregard the point of departure of biogenic living: the basic biological and psychological needs of man. Rodin, the great French sculptor, was intuitively on the right wave length when he exclaimed (upon viewing a miniature Chinese landscape painting for the first time), "What greatness in the smallness!" The principles of both greatness and smallness are vividly emphasized by the philosophy and practice of biogenic living in general, and by the miniature but versatile BELL in particular.

It is from the basic outlook of the science of Biogenics that I want to stress this important point: the traditional forms of dwellings, as well as the more modern type, and even the geodesic dome, all contain a lot of *superfluous space.* Every unnecessary cubic yard of space involves more building material, more labor, more expense, more maintenance, more heating, cleaning, repairing, more taxes, more depreciation, etc. Rodin was right. The real greatness is in the smallness.

Smallness, however, is not necessarily meanness. If small size were the only criterion, a windowless igloo, or one of those new, prefabricated, tiny, emergency dwellings would suffice (or a mobile home, for that matter). Smallness is one important factor; beauty, the true esthetic beauty of nature, is another. For too long the human dwelling has been an effort to cut ourselves off from nature; to over-protect

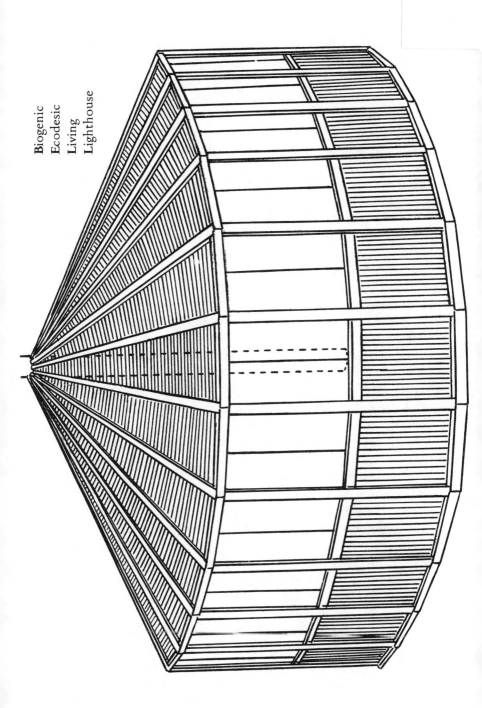

Biogenic
Ecodesic
Living
Lighthouse

131

ourselves from her and create as firm a barrier as possible against the intrusion of nature into our lives. Some architects of genius, like Frank Lloyd Wright, have created exteriors which beautifully blend with their natural surroundings; unfortunately, the interiors display all the drawbacks (mentioned above) of the traditional dwelling. A home should not be a decorator's showpiece or a status symbol; but just as we are an extension of nature and an integral part of it so should our dwelling be a natural and harmonious extension of ourselves.

Looking at the present situation, as we are squandering our natural resources and basic building materials, and inexorably running out of space, due to our uncontrolled catastrophic population growth, it is evident that a human dwelling shall contain only really necessary space and nothing superfluous. It is also evident that man is meant by nature to live as much as possible out of doors, and that our indoor space should consist mainly of necessary shelter and protection against the intemperances of nature, such as rain, excessive wind, cold, heat, etc. But of course this does not mean we should all move into tents and lean-tos, hastily constructed from odds and ends. The esthetic quality of our dwelling is extremely important. A human dwelling must be an integral part of nature and shall have a maximum of fresh air and light. It should not be wasteful of energy, it should have good tensile strength, and it should be safe in case of earthquake. It should not disrupt in any way the ecological balance of nature, nor disturb or detract from its immediate natural surroundings. It should also satisfy only our real needs and guarantee freedom from all kinds of superfluous expenses, such as large capital investments, mortgage payments, taxes, etc.

The Biogenic Ecodesic Living Lighthouse, known in Europe by its acronym of BELL (and introduced by me to various Essene and Biogenic communities in Europe during the twenties) is a miniature biogenic dwelling modeled after the master builder of nature: the honey bee—symbol of Creative Work to the ancient Essenes. The honeycomb is the perfect and most beautiful polygonal construction, the simplest, strongest, and most economical of all forms. The basic polygonal unit can be easily added to or multiplied in any combination or variation. One unit is perfect for the single person, a double unit for the couple, and a triple or quadruple unit for a family. It can also be used as a greenhouse, partially or totally, to satisfy the illogical building codes, the limitations of which were, fortunately, not faced by our hardy pioneer ancestors; otherwise, the United States would never have been successfully settled.

Simple, natural and creative living, in freedom and undisturbed solitude, is our inalienable birthright, given to us (in the language of our Declaration of Independence) by "the Laws of Nature and Nature's God." We, renascent Essenes, want to remind all good Americans, in the name of our Declaration of Independence, to safeguard through democratic processes these inalienable rights, for which our founding fathers fought so heroically, so that those immortal words written two hundred years ago may be an even brighter beacon to a free world.

THE BELL

This ideal of simple, natural, creative living is perfectly expressed in the miniature biogenic dwelling, the BELL. Its polygonal construction can easily be built by the average person, with simple tools. The basic building materials are easily obtained and are variable, according to one's financial resources and local availability. The dwelling can be adapted easily to different climates. Due to the tremendous savings in labor and materials, it is accessible to virtually everyone. It is resistant to earthquakes and strong winds. Because it is constructed of identical small parts, it is very easy to repair. It requires minimal property taxes, minimal maintenance, and no expense for utilities. The lot required is the smallest possible: only a hundred square yards which may include an additional 100 square yards for a miniature orchard and vegetable garden, with three outdoor assets: a Sumerian Bath (described in *The Chemistry of Youth*), a toilet, and a compost heap.

The BELL is a life-generating (with its indoor green garden) and human life-sustaining living unit utilizing light, heat, coolness, air, sun, water, and soil, for optimal human health, not interfering ecologically with the environment and able to recycle everything (vegetable by-products, waste paper, human solid and liquid by-products, etc.) into biodegradable, clean, useful substances belonging to the permanently moving Wheel of Life. Its shape and construction is simple and easy, it can be designed for one, two, or more persons, the cost is minimal, and to live in it in voluntary simplicity and spiritual awareness of nature, combined with intellectual creativity, leads to a symbiosis with Nature, the Spiritual, and Culture.

SYMBIOSIS WITH NATURE IN THE BELL

The BELL represents an organic, dynamic symbiosis with Nature. Living in it, we have the forces of Nature beneficial to man, on an optimal scale, and we avoid its excesses. The basic principle of the BELL is that of Protogoras of ancient Greece, who said that man is the measure of all things. The tenderness of moderate sunshine, moderate breezes, moderate temperature, etc., are all favorable to our well-being. The conventional house permits us only one-sided, partial adaptation to the different surrounding elements of Nature, from which it separates us. The BELL embraces the attributes of a living organism which can adapt itself adequately to unusual and unexpected changes in the environment. Let us examine a few of these adaptations.

Sunshine and Light. In hot weather we can avoid excessive sunshine by using the simple cotton curtains indoors, allowing to enter only the degree of light which is agreeable to us. On days with very little sunshine and light, by not using the curtains at all, the entire little dwelling becomes a transparent window, letting us enjoy the maximum of whatever light is available in nature. Or we can direct the light according to the seasons, letting in the sunshine from the southern windows in the winter, or from the northern windows in the summer.

Air. In hot weather we can leave open all the double windows, preferably those exposed to the cool breezes of the north. In cold weather, opening only the southern windows will let the warm air in. In moderate weather we can leave all the windows open all around, creating for ourselves the feeling of practically living out of doors.

Heat and Cold. The best heating and air-conditioning is

Nature herself. In moderate weather, we can leave open all the windows all around. In hot weather we open the northern windows for cool breezes, and in cold weather the southern windows for the warm air. In a cold wave we can close all the double windows and use the inside curtains, close the outside shutters, and finally, use in moderation the little wood stove. With all the airspaces and layers of insulation, you will find you need *very* little additional heating.

Rain and Snow. During summer showers we can open all the windows and enjoy the fragrant, moist air, full of vitality, listening to the soothing sound of rain as it refreshes and invigorates the air and soil. In winter, we remain warm behind the double glass while we open all the cotton curtains and enjoy the panoramic embrace of the white snowfall.

Sounds. If you live in the country, through your panoramic open windows you can enjoy the wonderful symphony of nature: the rustle of leaves in the wind, the murmur of the breeze-blown foliage of the trees, the ever-changing variety of birdsong, the more mysterious sounds of other wild creatures, etc. And if you still live in the noisy city, you can insulate yourself through your double windows, ceiling air spaces, even by your curtains and shutters in an extremely noisy part of the day, and enjoy silence, which according to Pythagoras, is the music of the cosmic spheres.

Colors and Shades. Unlike living in a conventional house, which effectively cuts us off from Nature, the BELL allows us to experience to the fullest the beauty of the changing seasons and the cycles of the day. You will be surrounded by a panorama of continuously changing colors and the kaleidoscopic movement of the clouds.

Fragrances. Unless you live in a polluted city, you will bask in the fragrances of nature, surrounding you in a continuously changing variety. If you live in the city, use only the necessary degree of cross-ventilation and keep several biogenic meadows and biogenic batteries around you in your dwelling to provide continuously generated natural oxygen from the fast-growing, oxygen-generating vegetation.

These represent just a few potentialities of a wonderful biogenic and psychogenic way of life in the BELL, most of which are missing in a stuffy, artificial, traditional house, based on a great number of unhealthy superfluities, instrumental of self-exploitation. Biogenic Living replaces this artificial anomaly with voluntary creative simplicity and material and spiritual freedom, based on the minimum of real needs.

THE PHILOSOPHY OF THE BELL

For tens of thousands of years our ancestors lived mostly in simple, peaceful dwellings, surrounded by nature. The DNA in our cells is programmed for a simple and peaceful environment, which we have dramatically, even recklessly, transformed into a pandemonium of modern technological living. Due to this profound conflict, the statistic of nervous breakdown and mental disease is increasing in geometrical proportion. Our senses, as well as our phylogenetic subconscious, programmed for a natural environment, revolt against the increasingly complex weight of our artificial, stressful way of life. The individual feels more and more disoriented, confused, without direction, because all the means to satisfy his basic individual needs are out of his control and he is helpless in an apparently irremediable slavery of social exploitation by big business, big unions, and big governments, as well as by his own self-exploitation: due to ignorance, he sacrifices real values, like health, time, and peace of mind, for superfluous and harmful things he does not really need. Instead of reading great books, an endless source of philosophical values and ethics for past generations, television and other media forms now provide him with instant news, instant entertainment, and instant ephemeral, artificial values, changing with every world development or passing fad. The structure of society may be more permissive, but the new absence of rules leads not to a sense of freedom, but only to confusion. The individual desperately needs to escape from this chimera of "the Grand Central Station," to the unfulfilled dream of a simple, natural, peaceful environment, for which his organism has been programmed through tens of thousands of years of phylogenetic heredity, and from which he gradually became exiled by a century of increasing madness. Subconsciously he is longing for Canaan, eager to make his exodus, but inexorably chained in the bondage of an Egypt of unemployment, crime, pollution, inflation, taxes, debts—all the miseries of life in an age of uncertainty—a life most often spent in constant fear of the unknown future.

Consider the BELL as a refuge, a declaration of independence from the Grand Central Station. If, for many possible reasons your exodus cannot be complete, consider it for your weekends and your vacations, as a preparation and training for your future, complete exodus. To maintain mental sanity in our progressively self-destructive world, everybody needs periods of peace and regeneration to recharge the batteries and satisfy our phylogenetic heredity and inner disposition. It is a frightening, even appalling thought to consider how many billions of dollars are spent by North Americans on tranquilizers every year, and even more frightening to consider what will happen when one day those tranquilizers will no longer be available. Instead of being dependent on pills, drugs, alcohol, and junk food to dull the pain of being alive during the latter part of the twentieth century—instead of fighting the madness and trying to conquer the world—we shall try to meditate, to find ourselves and the true meaning of life, which is still eternal and inviolate behind all the noise and confusion of the twentieth century. In a word, let us try to live periodically like an Essene, a disciple of Zarathustra, or a follower of Buddha thousands of years ago. We can happily and successfully remove ourselves from the madly revolving wheel of self-exploitation. In the miniature fruit and vegetable gardens of our BELL, we will become conscious of the changes in our air, sunshine, rain, soil, vegetation, and discover our unity with the Earthly Mother. What is more important, we will learn to draw from these sources of energy, harmony, and knowledge the power to regenerate ourselves. By spending our sacred hours contemplating the beauty of perennial nature and the masterpieces of universal literature, we will discover our title to nobility and become a child of nature—adopted into the real aristocracy of the great thinkers of all ages.

If escape from the city is not yet possible, and if you have the space, build the biogenic miniature dwelling as a little sanctuary somewhere in your garden, and take at least an hour's daily refuge in it, to keep your contact with Nature and the great philosophers. (The tea room of ancient Japan was an interestingly related effort to commune with nature and peace in a place set apart from the usual daily routine of material living.) It doesn't matter how much of a "city person" you think you are—it takes far more time than one generation to wipe out the programming of thousands and thousands of years. The DNA in your cells is longing for this periodic regeneration which (even if you use it only as a temporary refuge) will give you strength for your daily quixotic battle with the elusive windmills of the Grand Central Station. It will be a good training for survival through creative simplicity and self-sufficiency, a kind of insurance policy for probable and real future emergencies. It will be a bridge between your present haphazard way of living, and your possible, future, meaningful Canaan.

We recommend to plant a line of fruit trees around the BELL. During the summer they will shade the windows, and during the winter, as they lose their leaves, they will let in the sunshine. The windbreak so created is the most ancient energy-saving device. Exposure to the direction of prevailing winter winds will benefit considerably. This little dwelling, protected by a windbreak, uses 40% less energy during the winter than does an unprotected house. Until your fruit trees grow up, you may use a slatted fence, or something similar. The most effective location for a wind-break is upwind a distance of two times the height of the building. As prevailing winter winds come from a different direction than prevailing summer winds, a windbreak can be placed to divert winter wind away from the little dwelling without interfering with summer breezes. Blocking the wind will protect the wall layer of air from the scouring force of wind. Another idea: outside shutters that keep out heat or light are a valuable energy-saver, neglected or largely replaced these days by superfluous imitations that do not really work.

For simple cooking (the biogenic nutrition is 80% raw), an old-fashioned, but still very efficient, Aladdin mantle lamp can be used not only for light, but for heating water for herb tea, scrambling an egg, etc. At the very most, the Aladdin lamp uses about one gallon of kerosene a month. As far as heating in a cold climate, in view of the excellent insulation of the miniature biogenic dwelling, the little wood stove is needed only occasionally, using only waste paper and a tiny amount of wood. It will suffice perfectly for the small amount of cooking that cannot be done on the Aladdin lamp, an occasional simple cereal, soup, or cooked vegetables. The *small size* and efficient insulation simplifies everything.

For Further Reading:
The Biogenic Dwelling
Father, Give Us Another Chance

BIOGENIC MEDITATION

"Be strong, and enter into your own body:
for there your foothold is firm.
Consider it well, O my heart!
   go not elsewhere. . . .
Put all imaginations away,
   and stand fast in that which you are.
As the seed is within the tree,
   and within the seed are the flowers,
   the fruits, and the shade,
So the seed is within the body,
   and within that seed is the body again."
                                    —Kabir*

THE ANCIENT ESSENE COMMUNIONS
WITH THE NATURAL AND SPIRITUAL FORCES

Fragmentary records of ancient traditions which have come down to us show that over eons of time man has gradually begun to develop within his being a certain receptive apparatus through which he is able to absorb the currents of force flowing in and around him, and consciously utilize them as sources of energy, harmony and knowledge.

According to the Essenes, the development of these receptive centers was an essential part of one's individual evolution. They also considered that systematic and daily practice of a correct method was necessary for their development. This is why, in regard to our individual evolution, the practice of Biogenic Meditation is the most important of all the facets of biogenic living.

Through this practice, the subtle centers of the body can be opened and access given to the universal storehouse of cosmic forces. The purpose of this was to put the organs of the physical body in harmony with all beneficial currents of the earth and the cosmos, so they could be utilized for the evolution of the individual and the planet.

Luther Burbank: "In pursuing the study of the universal and everlasting laws of nature, whether relating to the life, growth, structure and movements of a giant planet, the tiniest plant, or the psychological movements of the human brain, some conditions are necessary before we can become one of

*from *Songs of Kabir,* translated by Rabindranath Tagore, available from the International Biogenic Society.

nature's interpreters or the creator of any valuable work for the world. Preconceived notions, dogmas, and all personal prejudice and bias must be laid aside. Listen patiently, quietly, and reverently to the lessons, one by one, which Mother Nature has to teach, shedding light on that which was before a mystery, so that all who will, may see and know. She conveys her truths only to those who are passive and receptive. Accepting these truths as suggested, wherever they may lead, then we have the whole universe in harmony with us. We discover we are part of a Universe which is eternally variable in form, eternally immutable in substance."

Another great genius in the study of plant life, George Washington Carver, said, "When I touch grass, I touch infinity. It existed long before there were human beings on the earth, and it will continue to exist for millions of years to come. Through the grass, I talk to the Infinite, which is only a silent force. This is not a physical contact. It is not in the earthquake, wind, or fire. It is the invisible world of nature of which I, too, am a part."

We shall remember that in our phylogenetic evolution, the involuntary organovegetative system is hundreds of thousands of years older than our voluntary cerebrospinal system, and also that it is much more powerful. We shall also acknowledge the fact that our cerebrospinal system is so inextricably enmeshed in the complexities and increasingly perplexing multiple aspects of our deteriorating environment, that it evidences more and more deterioration of its functions and stress alarms, parallel with erratic manifestations of psychological immaturity, without mentioning a succession of inadequate attempts to adapt to our increasingly chaotic environment. The voluntary cerebrospinal system has become a continuously disturbing source of disharmony and multiple pathology.

It is therefore self-evident, that when we disconnect the functions of the cerebrospinal system, a "pause that refreshes" will surely result. So far, so good. But this is only half of the solution. In the process of *biogenic meditation*, we not only disconnect this constant source of cacophonic disharmony and bewildering perplexity, but we also enter into a harmonious communion with the kingdom of the organovegetative functions, so that the primeval, cosmovital biogenic lifestream, will now undisturbedly, unhamperedly govern, completely independent of our voluntary, cerebrospinal processes, which we have sent on vacation. The organovegetative system governs superbly our unbelievably complex biopsychological functions, being a supergenius mathematician (knowing exactly how many millions of phagocytes, erythrocytes, and leucocytes, to create every minute), an equally supergenius biochemist, its inherent knowledge based on millions of years of phylogenetic experience. This homecoming to our primeval state not only disconnects our continuous source of troubles, but fills us with powerful biogenic forces performing multilateral biopsychological repairs. The cumulative effect of absorption of energies from this biogenic field of forces, creates, as an after-effect, a new feeling of well-being, which continues to work even after the duration of biogenic meditation (or more correctly, *communion,* is over.

Plants still exist in conformity with the organovegetative state, in a kind of permanent biogenic meditation. They are one with the earth, they live and breathe in perfect harmony with her—they do not break the Law. From the humble miracle of grass, to the splendor of the tallest tree, they are living exemplars of the cosmic order.

BIOGENIC MEDITATION

> . . . and worship the benignant meditations inspired by Asha, the Cosmic Order. . . and I pray that propitious results may be seen in the Living Grass. . .
>
> —Zend Avesta

Biogenic Meditation is the most important practice in biogenic living. For humans, *life* is the most important power on Earth. The most primeval and universal life-generating (biogenic) functions are the mobilization of life-forces in a seed, the appearance of embryonal germinates (sprouts), the birth and initial growth of a young baby plant, the capture of solar energy by the green leaves of the young plant, and its initial growth, which in the case of the simplest, but most vital plant on earth, the grass, takes place in about the first two or three weeks. During the *initial, rapid biogenic growth,* the little grass-plants—we may call them baby greens—provided the environmental preconditions of life (temperature, sunlight, humidity, quality of air and soil) are favorable, will manufacture large amounts of surplus energy, being in a biogenic condition and period of their lives. Soon, this surplus life energy becomes smaller and smaller, the speed of growth-rate slows down, and its life-forces gradually diminish and finally settle on a subsistence level, just enough for its biological needs (but having no surplus to spare)—this period is its *bioactive period.* With time, the plant gradually will have only a limited amount of vital energy, not quite enough to maintain its optimal biological function, the symptoms of which result in deficiency of chlorophyll, fading and dying leaves, the discontinuation of growth—this period is the stagnating, or *biostatic period*—we may call it old age. Finally, when its sources of nutrients or energies from the environment fall below even the biostatic level, according to the stored instructions of the DNA and RNA, the master computer inherited from its original seeds, the sad spectacle of *biocide*—death—occurs, and the biocidic remnants return to the terrestrial metabolism, the great equalizer.

The purpose of the biogenic meditation (more correctly, the biogenic, dynamic union with the primeval Ocean of Life) is to draw and absorb in a tactile way, biogenic—life-generating—life forces from the available surplus of the baby plant, which is possible only while the baby plant is in its biogenic phase (corresponding to the human puberty). Later, after it reaches the age of three or four weeks, the plant will not have any *surplus* life energy to spare.

The most vital and robust plant on Earth is the grass, with tremendous stamina to survive the most excessive cold and hot climates, covering the largest plant-inhabited area of our planet, and the most popular and easily accessible seed is the wheat (although many other whole grain seeds can also do well). During the course of the Great Experiment, which began in 1939 and lasted a third of a century, we always used wheat (which we harvested every year from our special wheat farms in Valle Redondo, only twenty minutes from the center

143

of our Great Experiment, Rancho La Puerta).

To create and utilize the above-mentioned surplus biogenic energy, we used a cup-size container, the most popular size, usually of the same diameter and height, which we filled with fertile, wet organic soil from our ecological health garden,* planted on its top a dense carpet of wheat grains (previously soaked for 24 hours, rinsed, and then sprouted for 24 hours. See the description of how to make a biogenic battery in a previous chapter.). The wheat-grain carpet in the container was sprinkled thoroughly (but not drowned), then covered with a small piece of plastic, or a small plastic bag, to retain the moisture until the little root-sprouts could find their way into the soil. Over the plastic we put a piece of paper to create darkness. After 12 hours we removed the covers and sprinkled the grains again gently (always avoiding the two extremes of dryness and drowning) and then replaced the them. In another 12 hours the covers were removed completely. After a short, sprout-like embryonal period, and a start of baby-like growth, giving enough water each day just to keep them moist, photosynthesis, capturing the sunlight, rapidly developed. The tender young leaves became green in 48 hours, and soon began their adolescent period.

While the initial growth of the young grass is *fast,* they are generating intensive biogenic energy and are capable through tactile transmission of sharing it with us.

Seven days after planting, the cup-size biogenic battery is ready for us to lay our hands on it, thereby drawing its biogenic energy to flow through the whole body. This communion of regeneration will draw us into a vegetative, primeval, vital communion with dynamic starbursts of biogenic energies. And this non-intellectual, non-notioned union has greater impact and regenerative power than any existing meditation technique. We feel the constant flow of biogenic energy through the whole body, and from time to time the regenerative flow through the spine will gently shake us. As we lose contact with the mental processes, we

*See *The Ecological Health Garden, the Book of Survival,* by Edmond Bordeaux Szekely, available from the International Biogenic Society.

enter the powerful organovegetative world of the very young, fast-growing green leaves, radiating primeval bio-genic energies.

When the young, biogenic plant reaches the seventh day, the fast-growing, deep green robust grass is about six inches tall, its roots completely filling the whole container in a tumescent, hard condition. Your biogenic battery is now ready for use.

To perform the biogenic meditation, place the plant on a table, about one foot from the edge. Sit easily on a comfortable chair, facing your biogenic battery. After a minute or two of relaxation, grasp with both hands, between your fingers, as if in prayer, the young biogenic grass plant, close your eyes, holding it for about twenty minutes (elbows resting comfortably on the table), feeling between your fingers the living, dewy freshness of the young plant, and feeling the biogenic life-forces entering into your whole body, through tactile contact with your biogenic battery. As it is very important to be comfortable for these twenty minutes, it will be a good idea to support your elbows on something soft (a quadrupled soft towel, for example). Also, let your palms rest easily on the rim of the container. If you want to think on a word at each breath, you shall use only the word "Life," because *it is, and it corresponds to the reality.* You will feel the surplus biogenic, life-generating forces from the vigorously-living young plant flowing con-tinuously into your whole body; soon after this flowing sensation, you will feel a tingling sensation, especially through your spinal cord, and finally, this powerful lifestream will shake your whole body from time to time. After about 20 minutes, open your eyes, remove your palms and fingers from the plant, rest for a few minutes, and, refreshed, proceed with your daily activities. Repeat the whole procedure once more in the evening, preferably sometime before dinner (never after meals) and not just before retiring, as the powerful biogenic energy absorbed may keep you awake for several hours.

This biogenic meditation will free you twice a day from the tyranny of our restless, tense, worrying cerebrospinal functions (the seat of your voluntary processes) and will keep you in contact exclusively with your organovegetative system—millions of years older and incomparably more powerful—working independently from your conscious, voluntary actions and mistakes. This primeval, infallible, supercomputer which performs every second for you the most complicated mathematical and biochemical calculations, knowing exactly how many millions of different cells (leukocytes, erythrocytes, phagocytes, enzymes, hormones, etc.) to synthesize in the thousands of cellular systems of your organism, is the omnipotent and omniscient Law of Life, directing all manifestations of Life on our planet.

Actually, this ancient practice is much more than simply a form of meditation: it is in reality an incredibly powerful biodynamic union and communion with the greatest and most ancient primeval power on earth. As Kabir, the great poet-saint of ancient India, said:

> . . . It has no end, nothing stands in its way.
> Where the rhythm of the world rises and
> falls, thither my heart has reached. . .

There are hundreds of different meditation methods in vogue, but these only temporarily free you from certain tensions and stresses, "connecting" you mostly with imaginary, unreal hypotheses, but not connecting you in an actual, tactile way with such a *real* and tremendous power as this *vital, life-generating, primeval lifestream.* While you practice the biogenic meditation only twice a day, the cumulative repetitive effect is constant, and affects your behavior twenty-four hours a day. You will soon discover that you feel refreshed, vital, full of energy, finding an inner peace and harmony with nature, society, and culture. You will experience a complete regeneration in feeling, thinking and acting, achieved by the security that you have permanent access to all the sources of energy, harmony, and knowledge. You may not know everything (remember what Lao Tzu said: "It is better to travel hopefully than to arrive"), but you will know all things which are necessary for happiness, and that is not an easy achievement. Happiness is difficult to find within ourselves, and impossible to find elsewhere.

"The heavens smile, the earth celebrates,
the morning stars sing together,
and all the Children of Light shout for Joy."
— *The Essene Gospel of Peace*
Books II and III

THE HORIZONS OF THE BIOGENIC, BIODYNAMIC COMMUNIONS WITH OUR PRIMEVAL SELF

"The moon shines in my body,
but my blind eyes cannot see it:
The moon is within me,
and so is the sun.
The unstruck drum of Eternity
is sounded within me,
But my deaf ears cannot hear it. . ."
— *Kabir*

The biogenic meditation in oneness with the cosmovital forces emanating from the tactile contact with the biogenic battery, not only brings our erratic cerebrospinal system into greater and greater harmony, through cumulative effect, with our inner and outer biogenic environment and functions, but also proves the efficiency of these biogenic meditations (communions), by producing measurable improvements in our psychophysiological states, more and more similar to biogenic functions. This beneficial switch from our tense cerebrospinal functions toward the peaceful, relaxed organovegetative hypometabolic state, produces palpable, plausible, and scientifically and quantitatively measurable facts:

1. During these biogenic communions, there is a considerable lowering of oxygen consumption (an average of from 250 to 210 cubic centimeters per minute, much closer to plant metabolism, enabling us to exist with less oxygen intake (which might be extremely important in an emergency).

2. We found also that carbon dioxide elimination was lowered (also much closer to biogenic plant metabolism) from 220 to 185 cubic centimeters per minute. This, in case of an emergency of being trapped in a closed space, also could prove very useful.

3. Both the rate of respiration (from 16 breaths per minute to approximately 9 per minute) and the volume of respiration were considerably reduced, representing a greater

oxygen economy, closer to plant-like behavior.

4. Our stress-created waste products, like blood lactate, etc., are very considerably decreased, little by little approximating the hypometabolic state of the relaxed, growing young grass.

5. Our high arterial pressure starts to gradually decrease, reaching a normal level, further indication of complete elimination of stress.

6. The heartbeat and pulse-rate become more and more normal, indicating a much easier, more effortless function of the heart.

7. Sensibility to pain is markedly lessened, another organovegetative plant quality.

In addition to the above scientifically measurable and verifiable facts, against which arguments have no value, we may add several mental achievements, *outside* of the duration of these biogenic meditations (communions), also similar to biogenic plant states and conditions. For example:

1. A state of relaxed alertness.
2. Improved concentration.
3. More adequate response to stressful conditions.
4. Faster and more adequate reaction time.
5. Increasing, then complete relief from insomnia.
6. Cumulatively less anxiety.
7. Gradual improvement of memory.

All the above improvements created by the continuous, uninterrupted daily biogenic meditations (dynamic communions with life-generating forces) amply indicate that our erratic, tense cerebrospinal functions are transformed into ever-increasing harmony with our primeval, phylogenetic organovegetative system, and the ancestral primeval affinity is reestablished. This potentially existing phylogenetic affinity makes it possible for us to achieve the above outlined improvements with only two daily twenty-minute meditation-communions, but with a constant, twenty-four hour a day *lasting* effect.

Here we may emphasize that nothing is inherently wrong with our cerebrospinal functions, provided we transform them into harmonious cooperation with our primeval organovegetative system. When cerebrospinal deviations are eliminated, the two systems form a harmonious unity. This is the great purpose of biogenic meditation.

Again, "meditation" is not really the correct term, nor can it begin to encompass the experience which awaits us through this practice. When we disconnect the activities of the cerebrospinal function—which is the superstructure of our being, enmeshed into the multiple chaos of the Samsara and violating the immutable laws of life and nature—we extricate ourselves from all anxieties, tensions, worries, and precarious perplexities of our artificial, complicated and dangerous environment, and return to and enter into a fundamental phylogenetic, dynamic *union* with the primeval cosmic and terrestrial Ocean of Life, freeing our suppressed organovegetative system from the tense, autocratic tyranny of the cerebrospinal system, like the prodigal son returning to his father's home and absorbing the Samadhi-like eternal sources of energy, harmony, and knowledge. This state of altered consciousness does not take us to Nirvana, but simply returns us to our own primeval, long-forgotten and rarely-experienced original Garden of Eden, from which we were exiled by our own deviation from the laws of the primeval, eternal, Cosmic Ocean of Life. The absorption of vital energies during this biodynamic communion is brief, but its cumulative daily effect is *lasting*.

For Further Reading:
The Four Volumes of the Essene Gospel of Peace
Biogenic Meditation
The Living Buddha
Toward the Conquest of the Inner Cosmos
Essene Communions with the Infinite

Praise be to Thee, O Lord,
For our mother, the earth,
Who sustains and nourishes us,
Bringing forth diverse fruits,
Flowers of many colors,
And the grass.

                         —St. Francis

BIOGENIC SEXUAL FULFILLMENT

"Biogenic fulfillment is pure poetry and beauty. It is self-evident and based on ageless wisdom and contemporary statistics, both little-known by perplexed humanity living at the end of the twentieth century."

—Aldous Huxley

Another domain of the science of Biogenics deals with the spiritualization of the sexual functions. These are very ancient traditions, and various teachings about them have come down to us from ancient India, ancient Sumeria and Persia, from the writings of Zarathustra in the Zend Avesta, from the Essene teachings, from the Plinius manuscript of Monte Cassino, and from many other ancient sources. Even in our present era, though we are sadly far from the intuitive knowledge enjoyed by our non-technological ancestors who lived on intimate terms with nature, there have been a few creative geniuses who dipped into the stream of these ancient traditions and wrote about them in unmistakable terms.

THE BIOSPHERE AND BIOGENIC ZONE OF EARTH

"The flow of electrons is fundamental to all life processes, of plants and humans. The electron magnetizes the chlorophyll in the plant cell, that makes it possible for the photon to become part of the plant as solar energy. The same magnetism draws the oxygen molecules into the continuously expanding chlorophyll cells of the plant. Electromagnetic energy is the most fundamental substance of all energy and matter and the indispensable component of all plant, animal and human life."

—Edmond Bordeaux Szekely: *The Tender Touch*

On our planet, we have a fairly large biosphere, the zone of life and all living organisms, which penetrates deep into the interior of the earth and goes high up in the atmosphere. This entire area is called the biosphere, but one specific central zone of it is by far the most important. This is the *biogenic zone,* the topsoil, the whole vast surface of soil over the planet, which is the meeting-place of all the different sources of energy: solar radiations, lunar radiations, stellar radiations coming to us from all over the galaxy and beyond—the energies of earth, such as water, air, sunlight, and all the minerals of the topsoil. Only here in the topsoil, on the surface of the earth, can be found the miracle of bacterial activity that makes all life possible on our planet. When we pick up a handful of topsoil, we have no idea how many thousands of microscopic microorganisms are teeming busily within it, invisibly doing their work. (Darwin wrote beautifully about this subject in his great classic on leaf mold, describing the earthworms and their role in the formation of topsoil on our planet.) There is something absolutely unique in that few inches of topsoil on the surface of the earth. Because it is a focal meeting-point of all terrestrial and cosmic energies, there is a vital exuberance of biogenic activity which is continuously creating vegetation. And particularly in the first few weeks of growth, they are full of *biogenic energy.* This is why the most important part of the biosphere is the *biogenic zone.* It is the seat of biogenic energy on our planet, and if for any reason it were destroyed, life would cease to exist. No human, animal or plant life could survive without that few inches of life-generating topsoil on our planet.

HUMAN BIOGENIC ZONES—EROGENOUS ZONES—LIBIDO—ORGASM

> *"Leaves of grass, stars and birds,*
> *Twined with the chant of my soul...*
> *Oh Life, immense in passion, pulse and power—*
> *Ocean of leaves of grass...*
> *Seed ethereal, the growth of seeds,*
> *and green leaves of grass..."*
> —Walt Whitman

In the human body there is also a biogenic zone, very similar to the biogenic zone of the earth in its concentration of life-generating force and vitality to create new organisms. This human biogenic zone is the product of the cooperation primarily between our glands and nerves, and between all the other different systems of the human body. Like all the other functions of the human body, this biogenic function is programmed in our cells by the DNA, condensing the phylogenetic experience of thousands and thousands of generations through hundreds of thousands and millions of years (if we take into consideration our ancestors on a lower level who preceded our species).

We also have the capability of continuously generating biogenic forces in our organism. If we utilize all the sources of energy and harmony in our environment and introduce into our organisms biogenic foods which contain in themselves that biogenic force of nature, then *our own generation of biogenic energies* will be strong and vital. But if we deviate from the laws of nature, inhaling all kinds of deteriorating substances in the environment and eating biostatic and biocidic foods full of chemicals and toxic by-products, *our own life-generating force* will definitely be impaired. This is one of the reasons why these days there is such widespread impotency in men and frigidity in women. We do not absorb all the sources of biogenic energy from our environment, neither externally nor internally through the right nutrition. Nevertheless, it is there—this life-generating power—because every cell in the human body is programmed for this function through hundreds and thousands of years of phylogenetic experience of an extremely long line of ancestors.

Wherever the organism produces these biogenic energies, these locations function like erogenous zones, which correspond to the vastly larger biogenic zone of our planet. In the human organism they manifest as *erogenous zones.* The sum total of biogenic energy produced in our organisms is the *libido,* the accumulated biogenic phylogenetic experience of thousands of ancestors, programmed indelibly in our human computer, the DNA in our cells. The *orgasm* is the discharge of this accumulated excess biogenic energy.

Regardless of all the different man-made names ascribed to various aspects of it, there is only one universal vital force which manifests in our planet, and *this same life-generating force which exists in the few inches of topsoil over the planetary biogenic zone, also exists in the biogenic zone of the human organism, as well as in animals and plants.*

ANCIENT TRADITIONS FROM THE DEAD SEA SCROLLS OF THE ESSENES

If we are to completely understand the spiritualization of the sexual function, we must go back to the purity and simplicity of the original idea, and remember that *the life-generating force field of the planetary biogenic zone is the same shared by the biogenic zone of our own human organism, and when we reach out and tap this vital, unlimited source of energy and harmony, we are performing a function which has been programmed into our cells by the wisdom of countless generations of ancestors—a* function which is absolutely necessary to our individual evolution.

The Essenes knew this when they uttered their communion with the Angel of Earth ("Angel" to the Essenes was a symbolic name for a cosmic or planetary force).

(The following is taken from my book, *Teachings of the Essenes, from Enoch to the Dead Sea Scrolls.*).

"The Essene communes with the Angel of Earth, saying: 'Angel of Earth, enter my generative organs, and regenerate my whole body.' As he says this, he contemplates the life-generating soil and the growing grass, feeling the currents of the Angel of Earth transform his sexual energy into regenerative forces.

"Earth represents the two aspects of the generative force which creates more abundant life on the planet. The one creates life from the soil, producing the trees, the grass, and all vegetation. The other manifests in human sexual energies. The individual is to understand and utilize the most optimal ways of growing plants and food, and of a harmonious sexual life."

This excerpt from my book indicates that the Essenes understood perfectly the quintessence of the ancient traditions regarding the affinity and symbiosis between the biogenic zone of the earth and the organs of generation in the human body. The ancient Vedic teachings, and many others, also recognized this practical identity, this harmony, this union between the two. When the communicant says, "Angel of Earth, enter my generative organs and regenerate my whole body," he is affirming the possibility of establishing contact between the biogenic power of the earth and the biogenic energy of the generative organs.

DYNAMIC PRIMEVAL INTERACTION
BETWEEN TERRESTRIAL AND HUMAN BIOGENIC FORCES

Of course, this contact between our generative organs and the few inches of biogenic topsoil over the face of the earth is not a direct one—we can no more translate this energy from the soil directly to our generative organs than we can assimilate nutritional energy by eating dirt. There must be a *bridge* between the biogenic zone of the earth and the biogenic zone of the human body, and *that bridge is the tender, young, fast-growing grass which has been brilliantly designed by the all-wise super-computer of nature to impart all the life-generating power of the primeval lifestream to the human body—through direct, caressing contact with the male and female generative organs.*

I will state again, as this point is extremely important, that this contact between the biogenic, or erogenous zones of the human body with tender, young, fast-growing vegetation, is nothing new. For hundreds and thousands of years our ancestors entered into the universal and primeval lifestream, an unlimited source of energy and harmony, through this contact between the young, biogenic plants and the human generative organs. And in these ancient traditions, it was the period *preceding* orgasm which was the most important—*a high plateau resulting in an intensive union with the biogenic lifestream of our planet, leading to an altered state of consciousness.* Nowadays, the achievement of a successful orgasm has reached an almost hysterical pitch, and is considered to be the badge of a healthy sexual life. But an orgasm is merely the physiological discharge of accumulated excess biogenic energy, something we share with every other member of the animal kingdom; homo sapiens have something superior, an added plus to nature. This something superior is our ability *to achieve spiritual union with the primeval lifestream of our planet—a lifestream which is our bridge to contact the Cosmic Ocean of Life. The intensive union achieved through caressing, gentle contact between the tender, young, biogenic grass and our generative organs takes place during the high plateau preceding orgasm, and not only during the orgasm itself, which is a purely physiological function.*

The most ancient traces of biogenic sexual fulfillment, according to the Plinius manuscript which I found in the Scriptorium of the Benedictine monastery at Monte Cassino, date back to the remote origins of the ancient Essenes. (The story of my discovery is described in my book, *The*

Discovery of the Essene Gospel of Peace.) According to Plinius, the ancient Essenes had a communion dedicated to the life, health, and vitality of the human body and of the whole planet, which brought about a dynamic unity between them. It taught the Essenes the role of vitality in their well-being, making them conscious of the life-forces in and around them, and enabling them to direct those forces toward their bodies with great intensity. It was this communion which gave the ancient Essenes their astonishing ability to absorb the vital life-force from tender, young plants, the grass of meadows, and trees. The words of this communion were: *"Angel of Earth, enter my generative organs and regenerate my whole body."* And with the enactment of this communion, one felt the life-generating forces of the growing grass, the primeval lifestream from the Angel of Earth, transforming sexual energies into regenerative forces.

These ancient traditions were not followed simply to achieve a physiological state of satisfaction of the erogenous zones. To the ancients, these practices were a bridge to enter into union with the sacred biogenic lifestream of the planet.

Now I would like to touch upon the practical aspects of biogenic sexual fulfillment, for an ancient tradition is valid only if it can help us in our individual evolution and make us an active, creative point in the universe. Let it be understood, first, that biogenic sexual fulfillment is not meant to replace sexual intercourse. Just as the great philologist, Dr. Zamenhof, created Esperanto not to replace the national languages, but to serve as a second, auxiliary language which everyone could use to better understand each other, so is biogenic sexual fulfillment to be used as an auxiliary method whenever regular sexual function is not practicable or desired. For those who enjoy healthy sexual functions, biogenic sexual fulfillment can be an avenue of union with the spiritual, primeval force of biogenic power. But for those who suffer disturbances in their sexual functions—unfortunately, the vast majority of men and women—biogenic sexual fulfillment, in addition to its ancient purpose, may be their only solution.

The misuse and abuse of our biogenic forces leads to all

kinds of disturbances, just as deviation from the basic rules of wholesome nutrition will create disease. The human body is an organic, dynamic unity of many functions, and violations of the laws of nature in one area will bring troubles in other areas—this is the law of inner microecology of the human body. The same confusion which exists today in the field of nutrition exists in the field of sexual functions, and it is getting worse all the time. Unwanted pregnancy, particularly among teenagers, is steadily on the rise, venereal disease is rampant in epidemic proportions, new infectious diseases are beginning to appear which as yet have no cure, and methods of contraception are either unesthetic, inadequate, barbaric (sterilization) or physically harmful (the Pill). No one knows the exact number of people experiencing dissatisfaction in their sexual lives, though experts say it has never been higher. Neither the stern repression of earlier times, nor the reckless permissiveness of the present era, have been able to normalize this troubled area of human life.

In the light of the science of Biogenics, the body's sexual responses are primeval, holy, and associated with the same life-generating forces which exist in the biogenic zone of the earth—a dynamic instrument of cosmic beauty and vitality. But both promiscuity and prudery profane these sacred feelings. Promiscuity brings with it not only the obvious dangers of disease, infection, unwanted pregnancy, and psychoneurotic problems, but also steadily erodes one's spiritual nature through constant contact with the confused and incoherent emotions of others. There is extreme vulnerability at the height of the sexual act, and when this vulnerability is exposed to inferior currents of thoughts and emotions, great damage can be done to the psyche. Prudery also cripples the true spirituality of the human sexual function by putting limitations and artificial barriers around what is "accepted" and "unaccepted" behavior. No matter how enlightened we think we may be, an aura of wickedness still hangs over the word "pagan," when we think of the ancient religious traditions that flourished before our present civilization, and it is still difficult, even for the most liberal-minded scientist, to dissociate the actual sexual response with the myriad of customs, practices, taboos, and traditions that accompany it.

When the human sexual response is focused on harmony with the biogenic, life-generating forces of the earth, and it is pursued in private, by an individual, with the entire being centered in truth and beauty, then there is no more beautiful celebration of the human spirit within the miraculous temple of the human body. When it is shared with another, a life companion of similar spiritual attitudes, then it is also beautiful. When it is squandered, or used for vulgar pseudo-pleasure, or promiscuous, or used as a tool of power, or a weapon, it becomes unspeakably destructive.

Undoubtedly, biogenic sexual fulfillment, as a method to prevent the tragedy of unwanted pregnancy, disease, and the twin evils of prudery and promiscuity, is extremely effective.

TACTILE REGENERATION AND ALTERED ORGASMIC CONSCIOUSNESS FROM BIOGENIC YOUNG GRASS

"The most beautiful thing we can experience
Is the mysterious.
It is the source of all true Art and Science.
He to whom the emotion is a stranger,
Who can no longer pause to wonder
And stand wrapped in awe,
Is as good as dead."

—Albert Einstein

The few remnants of the surviving literature of the ages, from the dawn of history through all ancient cultures, convey universal esoteric as well as exoteric traditions regarding the symbiosis between the generative organs of the human body and the biogenic zone of our planet. The same ideas always emerge from these writings: young, dewy green leaves of grass of the meadows possess a tremendous earthy generative power, obtained directly from the rays of the sun, the air, the water, and the nutrients of the soil, which, if absorbed through a gentle, tactile, caressing contact by our generative organs, will refresh and regenerate the whole body by establishing an intensive contact with the primeval Ocean of Life. This esoteric tradition is usually paralleled with the concomitant esoteric message that the spiritual result of this cosmovital communion with the primeval forces of Life is an altered, dynamic, orgasmic state of biocosmic consciousness.

"The tenderness of our flesh is born of the flesh of our Earthly Mother; whose flesh waxes yellow and red in the fruits of the trees, and nurtures us in the green grass of the fields and meadows. Man is the Son of the Earthly Mother; we are one with her. . . she is in us, and we in her.

—The Essene Gospel of Peace, Book One,
translated by Edmond Bordeaux Szekely

THE TENDER TOUCH

Sacred meadows of leaves of grass,
Nourished by mists of evening dew,
Delightful leaves and bud and blossom—
Embrace our limbs with fragrance. . .
—fragments from *Ode to Hestia*

With experience, we found that the best results in regenerative euphoria of a long plateau and altered orgasmic state of consciousness were achieved by following these rules:

1. The experience shall not be repeated more frequently than once a week.

2. The experience shall be performed individually, in complete privacy.

3. The experience shall not be performed when tired, tense, worried, angry or upset.

4. The experience shall not be performed right after eating, or right before sleeping.

5. The seeds and soil used to create the biogenic battery must be organic, free of chemicals, and very clean, to avoid any possible skin trouble.

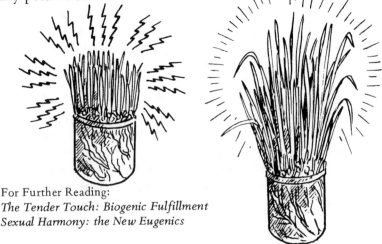

For Further Reading:
The Tender Touch: Biogenic Fulfillment
Sexual Harmony: the New Eugenics

BIOGENIC PSYCHOLOGY AND SELF-ANALYSIS

An unexamined life is not worth living.
—Socrates

THE ONE LAW

Before we explore in detail the practice of Biogenic psychology and self-analysis, let us look for a moment at the ruling principle in the lives, not only of the ancient Essenes, but of their spiritual ancestors, lost in the vastness of unrecorded history. This ruling principle, the foundation of their system of psychology and self-analysis, was the One Law—the totality of all laws in the universe.

Law is everywhere present. It is behind all that is manifest and all that is unmanifest. A stone falls, a mountain forms, seas flow according to law. In accord with law solar systems are born, evolve, and disappear. Ideas, sensations, intuitions come and go in human consciousness according to law. All that is, concrete or abstract, material or immaterial, visible or invisible, is ruled by law, the One Law.

The Law is formless as a mathematical equation is formless. Yet it contains all knowledge, all love, all power. The Law is life-generating—*biogenic.* It eternally manifests all truth and all reality. It is our teacher and friend, showing us all we must do, and know, and be to evolve to the beings we will someday become. The Law guides us in every problem, through every obstacle, telling us always the perfect solution.

THE INDIVIDUAL INVENTORY

Thousands of years ago, the Essenes practiced a system of self-analysis which enabled them to experience the unfolding of the One Law in every facet of their lives. The origins of this system are lost in the mists of time, but we know that a very similar system was used by the spiritual ancestors of the Essenes, the followers of Zarathustra in ancient Sumeria, and later in Persia.* Unlike modern methods of psychoanalysis, this ancient, life-generating, biogenic system of self-analysis is all-sided and universal—it has within it the Law which is the totality of all laws.

*See *The Essene Book of Asha* and *Archeosophy, a New Science,* by Edmond Bordeaux Szekely, both books available from the International Biogenic Society.

It represents a personal *individual inventory* of biogenic ideals of conduct and individual evolution, and can be of the greatest value to contemporary man as a kind of balance sheet of his degree of harmony with the Law.

The Essenes, considering as they did that man lives in the midst of a field of forces, knew that the natural and cosmic forces which surround him and flow through him are superior, positive, *biogenic* (life-generating) forces. But they also knew that man by his deviations from the law in thinking, feeling, and acting, constantly creates negative, inferior, *biocidic* (life-destroying) forces in the midst of which he also lives. He is connected with all of these forces and cannot be separated from them; moreover he is always cooperating, consciously or unconsciously with the superior, biogenic forces, or with the inferior, biocidic ones. He cannot be neutral.

Because it was so vitally important to cooperate with the biogenic natural and cosmic forces, the Essenes had a concrete program to help them in their task. Just as their spiritual ancestors, the followers of Zarathustra, had done centuries before, all the members of the brotherhood drew up a weekly balance-sheet of their activities during the past week, showing to what extent and in what respects they had either lived in harmony with the law, or deviated from it. The analysis helped them to recognize their strong and weak points. By sincerely and vigorously striving to make their thinking, feeling and actions ever better and better, they gradually progressed with the lifetime job of self-improvement. They were always aware of their duty toward each of the superior, biogenic forces, and they knew how these friendly forces could serve them as sources of energy, knowledge, and power. They knew it was necessary only to seek contact with them in order to receive more and more knowledge and energy from them. They were also aware that if they did not cooperate with the biogenic forces, they would cut themselves off from these sources of energy, harmony and knowledge, and thus cease to cooperate with the Cosmic Order.

There may be some who feel that with all our modern science and technology it is unnecessary to go back more than eight thousand years to an ancient teaching. But it is a question of how much the developments of science have accomplished in increasing human happiness and well-being. The general insecurity and neurosis of the present day and the widespread economic and social unrest give a definitely negative answer. Man has gained an enormous amount of theoretical knowledge in the framework of his scientific culture but this has not increased his happiness or individual evolution. It has not served to connect him with the universe, the cosmic order, or to show him his place and role in it. Without such knowledge, man cannot follow the path of optimal evolution for himself or for the planet.

The present day neurosis is caused by man's current deviations from the law of harmony with biogenic natural and cosmic forces. If a person tries his best to live in harmony with them he will never develop neurosis.

Psychology today tends to emphasize only one or two of these natural forces. Freud, for instance, considered deviations from the law of the natural force of sex caused man's inharmony; others have concentrated on other forms of deviation. But the system practiced in the time of Zarathustra and the Essenes considered harmony with *all* the biogenic natural and cosmic forces to be necessary for all-around health and psychological balance. Its superiority over other systems rests in its all-sidedness and universality.

The job of self-improvement, it shows, must be carried on day by day, by the individual himself. Despite the admonition of Socrates to "know thyself," very few people today have even the slightest degree of self-knowledge. People live in company of themselves all their lives without knowing the least thing about their real selves. There is no more complete way for someone to know himself—his strengths and his weaknesses, his values and deficiencies— than to follow this ancient system of self-analysis and make this individual inventory.

In contrast with the ancient method, which is done completely by the individual himself, modern psychoanalysis depends largely on the analyst, for the person being analyzed assumes a somewhat passive role. The Essenes believed that the individual's achievement of harmony is the lifetime task of the individual, not someone else's job to be completed in a couple of years or less.

THE SIXTEEN BIOGENIC FORCES

The sixteen biogenic forces used in the system embrace every aspect of human life. They correspond, in a degree, to the fourteen forces symbolized by the Essene Tree of Life.* It was not the purpose of the Essenes, nor Zarathustra, to divide the natural and cosmic forces into any rigid or artificial pattern, but simply to consider them in such ways as would express most clearly their value and utilization in human life.

Perfection was not demanded in the analysis, but the individual was urged to strive incessantly to improve his relationship to each of the sixteen forces and to achieve ever greater harmony and utilization of their biogenic powers and energies. The individual who does this will enjoy an actively creative life bringing him the highest measure of happiness and service to others. The one who continues to deviate will find life becoming less and less interesting and rewarding while misery and frustration will become increasingly great.

The teaching of Zarathustra about the Individual Inventory, a teaching also followed by the Essenes, provides a complete and practical guide in all the activities of life. If everyone today were to make the weekly balance, trying sincerely to cooperate with the One Law, manifested in the biogenic natural and cosmic forces, this would not be an age of neurosis, intolerance, wars and persecution. For the iron law of cause and effect teaches that, whether we wish it or not, we are always either cooperating with the Law or deviating from it. Behind the sixteen biogenic forces of this ancient system lies the wisdom of thousands of years, and that wisdom is as important today as in the past.

Of the sixteen biogenic forces that were utilized in making the analysis, eight belonged to the earthly forces and eight to the cosmic ones. The earthly forces were *sun, water, air,*

*See *Teachings of the Essenes from Enoch to the Dead Sea Scrolls,* by Edmond Bordeaux Szekely, available from the International Biogenic Society.

food, man, earth, health, and *joy.* The cosmic powers were *power, love, wisdom, the preserver, the Creator, eternal life, work,* and *peace.*

According to the ancient teachings, man has a thinking body, a feeling body, and an acting body. Our thoughts, our feelings, and our actions all must act in harmony if we are to cooperate with each natural and cosmic force. This is why the Code of Zarathustra contained only six words, yet it was more all-encompassing than the thousands of man-made, contradictory laws we have today; it was simply: *Good Thoughts, Good Words, Good Deeds.* According to Zarathustra, and the Essenes, in order to truly cooperate with each biogenic force, we must not only understand it thoroughly in our minds, not only desire with all our heart to feel its reality, but we must also perform with our bodies the actions necessary to accomplish its purpose.

Therefore, the analysis considered each of the forces from three different aspects, and these were the questions asked of each individual, by himself:

1. Do I understand this power or force?
2. Do I feel the significance of the force deeply and sincerely?
3. Do I use the power continually and in the best possible way?

THE BIOGENIC EARTHLY FORCES

The *Sun* is a very important source of energy and its solar power is to be contacted and utilized to the utmost every day in the form that is best for the health and well-being of the individual.

Pure *Water* is an essential element of life. It is to be used in the proper way in biogenic nutrition, and a bath in water is to be taken every morning throughout the year.

Pure *Air* has a tremendous role in the health of the body, and as much time as possible is to be spent outdoors breathing pure, fresh air and utilizing the energies of the atmosphere for health.

Food should be biogenic and bioactive (see the chapter *Biogenic Nutrition*) and taken in the right amount to supply another vital force to the organism. Food, water, and air are the elements most vulnerable to contamination in our present day, and we should be constantly alert and strive incessantly to maintain to the best of our ability the purity of these elements as they enter the body and create the preconditions for optimal utilization of the other biogenic forces.

Man was considered to be a force representing each one's right and responsibility toward his own individual evolution. Every person is to use every moment to further his progress in life and it is a job which no one can do for him. He is to know, and understand, his own potentialities and find the most practical way of developing and utilizing them in the service of mankind. To man is given the most sacred role of all: that of co-creator with God, and he must seek the optimal ways to fulfill that hallowed right and duty.

Earth represents the two aspects of the Biogenic force which creates more abundant life on our planet. The one creates life from the soil, producing the grass, the trees, and all vegetation. The other manifests in the sexual energies in man. The individual is to understand and utilize the most optimal ways of growing plants and food, and of the principles of biogenic sexual fulfillment, creating a harmonious sexual life.

Health is dependent upon man's harmonious relationship with all the forces of earth—with the sun, water, air, food, man, earth, and joy. The individual is to realize the importance of good health for his own sake and for the sake of others; and he is to practice all ways of improving his health, in thinking, feeling, and acting.

Joy is man's essential right, and he is to perform all his daily activities with a deep feeling of joy surging within him and radiating around him, understanding its great importance for himself and others. Joy is not an abstract emotion; it is a physical force with immense power to influence those around us, just as the glorious music which Beethoven wrote in his Ninth Symphony to Schiller's *Ode to Joy* has the power to stir the hearts of those who hear it.

These are the Biogenic forces of nature which man is to learn to understand and utilize. The following eight Biogenic powers of the cosmos are even more important in man's life, for he cannot live in complete harmony with the earthly forces unless he is also in harmony with the cosmic forces.

THE BIOGENIC COSMIC FORCES

Power is manifested continually through man's actions and deeds, both of which are the result of his cooperation or lack of cooperation with all other powers and forces, in accord with the iron law of cause and effect. The individual is to understand the importance of good deeds; he is to realize that his personality, position and environment in life are the result of his past deeds, even as his future will be exactly what his present deeds make it. He is therefore to strive at all times to perform good deeds that express harmony with the laws of both nature and the cosmos.

Love is expressed in the form of gentle and kind words to others, which affect the individual's own health and happiness, as well as that of others. Sincere love toward all beings is to be manifested by harmonious feelings and words.

Wisdom is manifested in the form of good thoughts, and it is man's privilege and right to increase his knowledge and understanding in every way possible so that he may think only good thoughts. He is to seek to grow in wisdom so as to understand more and more the cosmic order and his role in it. Only by attaining a degree of wisdom is it possible for an individual to learn to hold only good thoughts in his consciousness and to refuse to entertain negative, destructive thoughts about any person, place, condition, or thing. The Essenes believed we should always try to strengthen what is good in everyone and everything we contact; by doing this, and ignoring what is bad, the bad will become weaker and weaker and finally disappear entirely. This is the practical reality of wisdom.

Preservation of values concerns the power to preserve all that is useful and of true value, whether a tree, plant, house, relationship between people, or harmony in any form. When anyone destroys, or lets any good thing go to waste, deteriorate or be damaged, whether material or immaterial, he is cooperating with the negative, biocidic, destructive forces of the world. This is the foundation of what we know today as ecology, and every opportunity is to be used to prevent

167

damage to whatever has value, particularly the irreplaceable, precious natural resources of our planet.

Creation signifies the necessity for man to use his creative powers, since his role on the planet is to continue the work of the Creator. He is therefore to try to do something original and creative, something new and different, as often as he can, whether it is an invention of some kind, a work of art, or anything which will benefit others. The creative principle is of great importance in this ancient concept, since all other values flow from it.

When we start to contact the primeval lifestream of our planet, through the practice of Biogenic Meditation, then little by little we build a bridge to *Eternal Life.* This ultimate mystery, at once so simple and complex, is represented in the Individual Inventory by sincerity—man's sincerity with himself and others in all he does and with all those whom he meets. The Essenes believed that sincerity—the ability to evaluate oneself honestly without rationalizing or justifying the things one does or says or thinks—is, above all else, the path which leads to Eternal Life.

Work is the precondition of many other values. It means the performance of one's daily tasks, whatever they may be, with care and efficiency. Work is an individual's contribution to society and a precondition of happiness for all concerned, for when one person does not perform his work properly, others have to do it. "Happy is the one who has found his task; he should not ask for any other blessing."

Peace is to be created and maintained by every individual within and around himself. Since the condition of the whole of humanity depends on the condition of its atoms, each individual is to feel deeply the need for this inner peace and do all he can to establish and maintain it wherever he is. The great peace of the Essenes teaches man how to go back, how to take the final step that unites him with the cosmic ocean of biogenic power of the whole universe and reach complete union with the totality of all law, the One Law. This was the ultimate aim of all Essenes and governed their every thought, feeling and action. It is the final aim which all mankind will one day achieve.

The sixteen biogenic forces of nature and the cosmos, and their shadows, arrayed on the sixty-four light and dark squares of the Tapestry of Asha, of Zarathustra. This most ancient of all world pictures, the spiritual soil in which the roots of the Essene Tree of Life are planted, is fully described and explained in *The Essene Book of Asha*, by Edmond Bordeaux Szekely.

For Further Reading:
The Essene Book of Asha
Archeosophy, a New Science
Essene Communions with the Infinite
The Biogenic Revolution
The First Essene
Teachings of the Essenes from Enoch to the Dead Sea Scrolls

BIOGENIC EDUCATION

"Everyone receives two kinds of education:
the one given him by someone else,
and the other, far more important,
which he gives himself."

—*Edmond Bordeaux Szekely*

THE SEVEN DEPARTMENTS OF STUDY

The most important and most tragicomic deviations from the law of life in our present educational system which governs and directs the study of millions of people in every country, are the following:

First: They consider that the most important purpose of education is to compress in the minds of the students as much classified knowledge as possible during the few years of formal education.

Second: They isolate and segregate a group of people in a certain artificial medium, separating them completely from the real medium of study—life itself—and create artificial conditions and environments in which they pursue their studies. This is a second deviation from the law because the best medium for study and education is our natural medium, life itself, and not a certain campus or a certain department of an educational institution.

The third great deviation from the law is the erroneous consideration that the job of study is one or three or four or five or six years in a college or university. Study is a lifetime job. Life permanently creates new problems and needs in every age of human life. The real education is to learn how to deal with these problems, and to learn how to satisfy all the needs created by these different periods of life.

The ideal life is not one without problems—that would be extremely monotonous and very disadvantageous for our individual evolution and the development of our individual abilities. The ideal life is one full of problems, but with the knowledge of how to solve them.

We shall reformulate our basic ideas on study and education. As the present orthodox system of education becomes too static, too one-sided, and much below the tempo of development of contemporary life, there is a certain amount of dead weight in the form of petrified traditions and dogmas in our educational system. The real study and education shall have a completely different approach from that which we have at present.

First, we shall consider that education is not a one-sided action which, in the frame of a class, the professor does for the student, but is a bilateral, dynamic collaboration and cooperation between teacher and student.

Second, we shall consider that the basic purpose of education is to enable students to solve their individual problems in the different areas of their lives. Education must be individual and adapted entirely to the individual. "Man is the measure of all things," said the Greek philosopher Protogoras, and in the field of study, the student is the measure of all things. Education must not be a mass production in which every student, without consideration of his individual tendencies and hereditary dispositions, studies the same textbook and goes through the same schedule of studies and classes. This is another deviation from the law.

Study and education cannot be organized on a mass production basis as we have in our present educational institutions, which often resemble huge factories. It must be completely individualized to serve the individual in solving his basic problems in the different departments of life. In taking into consideration this basic principle of the new system of education we have divided study into seven departments. These seven departments are grouped from the central viewpoint of the problems of the individual as he or she has to face them in life. We deal with seven departments of life and the problems with which all of us are faced and which we must solve. In brief, the seven departments of study are as follows:

1. The first deals with the problem of health and the prevention of disease. This is a basic need of the individual and covers the basic problems which he has to face and solve. The technique of a healthy life, using the principles of Biogenic Living to maintain good health and prevent disease, is a very important vital knowledge which is and shall be translated into action in the individual's life. An unhealthy

person cannot be an active point in the universe, nor can he carry out his most important task: to continue the work of creation on this planet as co-creator with God.

2. The second department is professional orientation and vocational improvement. Each of us has a certain talent or vocation and each shall attain excellence and the optimum in his profession for his own good and the good of humanity.

3. The third department is that of leisure and creative hobbies. Outside of our profession we should have certain hobbies for self-expression and a channel for excess energies. Contemporary man greatly deviates from this basic law of life and his life becomes progressively mechanistic, based on a certain automatic repetition of daily schedule without the necessary periods of relaxation and leisure. For instance, reading great books (see the list in my *Books, Our Eternal Companions*), writing, the different arts, music, dramatics, travel, handicrafts, healthy outdoor activities, and most important, gardening; all these manifestations of life contribute to its fullness. In my books *The Chemistry of Youth* and *The Tender Touch,* I describe all the details of how to create and maintain a thriving mini-garden of baby greens and sprouts, which is not only a wonderful hobby for any age but also an invaluable contribution to one's health and vitality. On a larger scale, the independent, self-sufficient creative biogenic homestead can be a hobby for the whole family, and a way of life as well. On this subject, I recommend the study of my book *The Ecological Health Garden, the Book of Survival.* No adequate educational system can omit this aspect of life: leisure and creative hobbies.

4. The fourth department is family life, sexual harmony, eugenics and child psychology. This department of life is a very important one and every individual sooner or later is faced with the necessity of solving these basic and vital life problems. An adequate educational system must deal with these problems in order to give the individual adequate knowledge to solve them. This department is very important because, just as we have a chaos in professional orientation, we also have a similar chaos in contemporary family life, in sexual life, in eugenics and in the psychology of children.

The psycho-physiological improvement of the individual is a duty not only to himself but to humanity. In this field, knowledge of Biogenic Sexual Fulfillment could be an indispensable tool in the solution of many sex-oriented problems.

5. The fifth department of knowledge is the department of social cooperation and community life. The basic principles of cooperation between human beings have an extraordinary importance in our age, more than in any previous age. In a world in which the vastest distances are spanned in hours, we must recognize the fact that our planet is in reality one gigantic community, where the action in one part of the world can affect almost immediately, for better or worse, the lives of people living thousands of miles away. A far more adequate educational system must develop the tendency of cooperation instead of competition, which now forms the base of our present system of education. Our very survival depends on whether great nations will be able to cooperate instead of competing with each other. The fate of humanity is in the hands of our teachers and educators. If they are able to emphasize the extraordinary importance of cooperation and the cooperative spirit, and to decrease the tendency of competition and the competitive spirit that is so prevalent in modern life, they may be able to save humanity. This is why the department of social cooperation and community life is so important. The gradual development of centralization in Western civilization has progressively disorganized the little communities which previously existed in every country. One of the reasons for the tragic rise in drug use and alcoholism among young people is the steady disintegration of the small community, and within the community, the family unit. These frameworks of human cooperation have almost entirely disappeared and instead we have an exclusive centralization of life based on the competitive tendency of the individual. Messages on bumper stickers on fast-moving cars along freeways have replaced the give-and-take of small communities, fast disappearing from rural areas as urban sprawl eats up more and more agricultural land. This condition contains the seed of serious troubles in the future, and we already feel

the disastrous consequences. One of the most important duties of an adequate educational system is to deal with this problem.

6. The sixth department of life with which an adequate educational system must deal is the right method of thinking. As thought is the greatest power in the universe, the right method of thinking is the most efficient instrument to achieve our purpose in life. Our present educational system is only interested in using the mind as a storehouse of often irrelevant facts, figures and information. The best educated person is not the one with the widest knowledge, but the one with the best method of thinking. For it is possible to know everything and yet know nothing. It is not the quantity of knowledge which matters, but the method with which that knowledge is applied. It is important to penetrate into the essence of the correlations of phenomena with all-sided understanding if we are to solve the overwhelming problems of this latter part of the twentieth century. This essential department of life, the right method of thinking, does not have nearly enough attention from our present educational institutions and should be one of the most important departments of the new education.

7. Finally, the seventh department of knowledge concerns the spiritual aspect of life and the great philosophical and sacred teachings of all ages. A well-balanced world concept, in which the individual knows his place in the universe and life, is a solid foundation on which he can firmly stand in all adversities and in all critical periods of human history. But this spiritual education must be all-sided, all-encompassing, and void of dogma and discrimination. The practice of Biogenic Meditation, through which the individual enters the primeval and eternal lifestream of our planet through contact with tender, young grass, containing all the immense power of the Biogenic Zone of earth, is just as important to spiritual development as the study of the Dead Sea Scrolls or the *Tripitaka* of Buddha. Spiritual education must lead, not to a sectarian viewpoint, but to a lofty outlook which embraces all truth as equal and all human beings as brothers and sisters. One of the basic preconditions of an adequate

educational program must be to help the individual reach this harmonious, well-balanced world concept.

Thus we formulate a new system of Biogenic Education on the basis of giving adequate knowledge and help to the individual so that he can most adequately solve his problems in these seven basic departments of life. This basic formula forms the foundation of a new educational system and program of our ideal school of the future.

Biogenic Education, to use a phrase inspired by Lincoln, is education *of Life, by Life,* and *for Life.*

Of Life, because Life is our primeval quintessence, our real being, our greatest reality.

By Life, because real education can be acquired only through empirical life-experience, not in artificial milieux.

For Life, because the main purpose of education is to make us acquire all the knowledge, experience and skill which is essential for our health, happiness and creativity.

Therefore, we may conclude that the purpose of Biogenic Education is the teaching of and the training in the art of Biogenic Living.

Seminars and Workshops of Biogenic Living should consist of a series of lectures and demonstrations (with large drawings, three-dimensional miniatures, and work sheets with questions, etc.) about the following material:

First Lecture:	Biogenic Living in World Perspectives
Second Lecture:	Biogenic Nutrition and Gardening
Third Lecture:	Biogenic Living
Fourth Lecture:	Biogenic Dwelling
Fifth Lecture:	Biogenic Meditation
Sixth Lecture:	Biogenic Sexual Fulfillment
Seventh Lecture:	Biogenic Psychology and Self-Analysis
Eighth Lecture:	Biogenic Education

For Further Reading:
The Art of Study: the Sorbonne Method
Creative Work: Karma Yoga
The Evolution of Human Thought
I Came Back Tomorrow
Teachings of the Essenes from Enoch to the Dead Sea Scrolls

THE ALL-SIDED MICROCOSMOS
OF THE BIOGENIC BATTERY

THE GREATNESS IN THE SMALLNESS

For the benefit of those who may consider, even after all the material in this book, that the Biogenic Battery is still, simply, just a cup-size container of soil filled with growing wheat grass, I would like to describe, in simple terms, the immense and profound significance of that miniature biogenic forest we can hold in our hands. Just as Zarathustra was able to find the universe in a grain of wheat,* so can we discover every one of the sixteen natural and cosmic forces in the Biogenic Battery.

This idea is not new. In the manuscript found at Monte Cassino, Plinius, the Roman natural historian, described how the Essenes always had a few benches in their dwellings where they kept small earthenware pots, and in these pots were growing ordinary herbs and grass. These fast-growing herbs were not used only for eating, according to Plinius. The Essenes considered that the dense mini-forest they cultivated in the earthenware pots was a representation of the Cosmic Order, and they used them in their communions to remind them of the totality of the Essene teachings and traditions.

Sun is represented in the Biogenic Battery through the green color of the leaves of grass. The green color is chlorophyll, produced by photosynthesis, made possible only by the presence of sunlight. We see the power of the sun through the beautiful green color of the living grass.

Just as no organic life can exist on our planet without the sun, so would all life perish without *Water*. In this exuberant growth of tender young greens, there is more than seventy percent of that wonderful water of life of the Essenes. When we touch the grass with our hands we can feel the dewy freshness of the water-blessed living grass.

Regarding *Air*, the Biogenic Battery is like a factory of intensive manufacture of oxygen. Particularly in its biogenic stage, it is producing constantly the purest form of air for

*The beautiful legend of Zarathustra and the grain of wheat is told in *The Essene Book of Asha* and *The Essene Teachings of Zarathustra.*

176

our benefit, continuously cleansing and refreshing our immediate atmosphere.

As far as *Food* is concerned, the Biogenic Battery *is* food— of the purest, most nutritious kind. When the leaves are only three inches high, we can cut them and mix them with a vegetable salad, a cereal, or any other wholesome dish. The tender leaves of grass are bursting with vitamins, minerals, enzymes, and plant hormones.

Earth is also right here in the Biogenic Battery, for it is earth which provides the nourishment so the leaves of grass can grow. This little handful of soil contains all the elements, all the material preconditions for the growth of this green grass. Before our eyes we watch the miracle of birth as the wheat grain swells, the roots start their journey downward

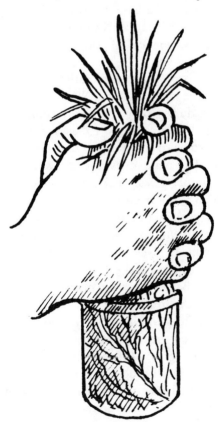

to draw life from the soil, and the sprout bursts open with a tender shoot of vivid green, bravely overcoming gravity in its upward ascent.

Health is nothing else but the dynamic unity of all the other earthly forces. There is nothing healthier than young, fast-growing grass—it is a true representation of health, as it unites all the forces of sun, water, air, food, earth, and joy.

Joy is a force one can experience through the practice of Biogenic Meditation. When we place our hands around the tender, young, living blades of grass, we feel the joyful exuberance of the primeval lifestream. Waves of joy surge through us and penetrate our bodies through tactile contact with the force field we share with the biogenic grass.

The first of the spiritual forces is *Power*. Kirlian photography has proved what the Essenes always knew intuitively— that fast-growing, biogenic grass has an intensive force field around it—tangible evidence of the life-generating power inherent in the living grass.

Love is another force which is experienced through tactile contact with the Biogenic Battery. When we hold the grass between our palms during Biogenic Meditation, a tremendous amount of excess energy flows to us from the Biogenic Battery. This gift to us of its energy is love—in its most direct and selfless form. The plant does not ask us if we are worthy or unworthy—it simply gives, unconditionally, of that magnificent energy which flows from the primeval lifestream of our planet through every living thing. There is a saying of ancient India: *only he gives, who gives himself.* This is what the little green plant is doing—it gives itself, its excess energy, to us. There can be no more beautiful example of love.

In the Biogenic Battery is the manifestation of infinite *Wisdom*. The coordination, the total preconditions, the utilization of all sources of energy, harmony and knowledge are here in this living grass. As George Washington Carver said, "When I touch grass, I touch infinity." And it was Einstein who said, "He who does not feel awe in contemplation of leaves of grass is as good as dead; it is a manifestation of supreme wisdom." Goethe, perhaps, put it best of all: "Gray are all the theories, but green is the tree of life." This little Biogenic Battery *is* the Tree of Life.

Preservation, the foundation of ecology, is perfectly represented by the Biogenic Battery, for nothing is wasted in this little growing forest of grass. Everything is utilized, everything is absorbed, everything is preserved. Even in its final phase of life, the elements of the plant return to the soil and provide minerals for future generations of plants. It is a living example of the moving wheel of life and the teaching of Buddha that "nothing is lost in the universe."

Now we come to the most important force, that of the *Creator.* Could anything be more apparent? The Biogenic Battery is the creation of life before our eyes. Biogenic means life-generating, and here is the generation of life. We cannot help but be reminded of the Creator every time we see the miracle of creation take place in the Biogenic Battery.

Eternal Life is also evident in the Biogenic Battery, because it is the most evident characteristic of the humble grass, which defies the law of gravity by growing anywhere and everywhere, even between cracks in bricks, cement and concrete. Grass was here on our planet fifty million years before us, and it will probably be here for more than fifty million years after us. For life is not the exclusive privilege of our planet, which is a tiny point in our solar system, which is a tiny point in our galaxy, which is a tiny point in the ultra-galactic system, which is a tiny point in the known universe, and an even tinier point in the unknown universe. Therefore, it would be megalomania to think that life exists only on our planet. Life exists on billions of other constellations, for the universe is a mind-staggering infinity. And we are not the only children of the cosmos. We may say we are the grandchildren of the cosmos, and children of our planet. And between all the other cosmic grandchildren in the infinite cosmic space there is a solidarity of all forms of life. This solidarity between all forms of life on innumerable planets, according to the Essene traditions, is the Cosmic Ocean of Eternal Life. Planets may disappear, solar systems may disappear, but the Cosmic Ocean of Life is eternal. And on this planet where we live, there is no more perfect representation of the Cosmic Ocean of Life than the fifty-million-year-old grass. When we touch the grass, we truly touch infinity.

Work, creative work, is also a force very much in evidence. A seven-day-old Biogenic Battery is a wonderful example of intensive, creative work. We can practically see the roots in movement, the leaves growing before our eyes. A week ago this was just a few grains of wheat, and now we see the lush green evidence of intensive, creative work—a wonderful example for us in our lives.

Peace is yet another force which we experience during the Biogenic Meditation, as if the little plant will share its most important secret with us only if we put forth our best efforts. Through our diligent practice of Biogenic Meditation, little by little we are able to put out of our minds the "Grand Central Station" of the twentieth century, all the harsh invasion of technology and man-created cacophony. Then, at last, we are one with the Peace of Nature, with the great primeval peace of the biogenic lifestream.

There is one force I passed over in its proper place because I wanted to mention it last: the force of *Man,* the co-creator with God. In the beautiful Essene symbolism of the Tree of Life, man is shown in the center, half of his body connected to the earthly forces, and half connected to the cosmic forces—a meaningful illustration of the idea that man unites in his body and spirit all the forces of nature and the cosmos in perfect harmony. When we practice Biogenic Meditation, we personify that symbol, for *we are here* in the center, physically here in the center of all these forces, our hands between the roots of the earthly forces and the grassy leaves of the cosmic forces. This is the role of man, to be surrounded perpetually by the natural forces and the spiritual powers; in the words of Tolstoy, "Man is not alone in the universe—he is surrounded by infinite powers of love and wisdom." When we practice Biogenic Meditation, we are not just symbolically in the center of an imaginary tree of life—we are effectively here—we touch all these powers as only we, as human beings, have the right to do—and the Tree of Life becomes a tangible reality, a Biogenic Battery between our hands.

This is the meaning of the earthenware pots which the Essenes kept filled with fast-growing herbs and grass. As a representation of the totality of the laws of the universe, of all the natural and spiritual forces and our unity with them, it was a constant reminder for them to live like the Tree of Eternal Life. And so it should be for us.

"I have reached the inner vision
and through Thy spirit in me
I have heard Thy wondrous secret.
Through Thy mystic insight
Thou hast caused a spring of knowledge
to well up within me,
a fountain of power,
pouring forth living waters,
a flood of love
and of all-embracing wisdom
like the splendor of Eternal Light."

—*From Enoch to the Dead Sea Scrolls*
by Edmond Bordeaux Szekely

For Further Reading:
Books I, II, III and IV of the Essene Gospel of Peace
The Essene Science of Life
The Chemistry of Youth
The Tender Touch: Biogenic Fulfillment
The Essene Book of Asha
Teachings of the Essenes from Enoch to the Dead Sea Scrolls

SEARCH FOR THE AGELESS

A monumental autobiographical synthesis, in three large volumes, of the literary, scientific and practical achievements of Edmond Bordeaux Szekely, documenting more than half a century of immense accomplishments. The three volumes contain 724 pages and more than 320 illustrations.

Volume One: MY UNUSUAL ADVENTURES ON THE FIVE CONTINENTS IN SEARCH FOR THE AGELESS. The title is the best description: one is mesmerized by the stranger-than-fiction autobiographical adventures of the author, from the Vatican and the Sorbonne, through the High Carpathians, India, the Plateau of Pamir (home of the fabled Hunzas), Central Africa, the South Seas, to California, Mexico, Central America, and the Northern Territories of Canada—all in search for the ageless. Interspersed with this fascinating material are the results of philosophical, ethnological, and archeological research, all with profound practical significance.   7.80

Volume Two: THE GREAT EXPERIMENT. The author's autobiography continues, leading the reader from the beginnings of the Great Experiment (33 years, 123,000 participants, with thousands of lectures by the author, as well as many more thousands of individual consultations) to its fulfillment in the reorganization of the International Biogenic Society, founded by the author and Nobel Prize-winning author Romain Rolland in 1928. Packed with fascinating photographs and illustrations, *The Great Experiment* is impossible to put down, once started.   8.80

Volume Three: THE CHEMISTRY OF YOUTH represents the comprehensive, condensed results of half a century of medical practice and research on a universal scale, translated with creative simplicity into a clear, all-encompassing guide to the prevention of disease and the preconditions of a healthy, long life. To describe its contents—the factual, scientific, revolutionary results of the Great Experiment in the fields of ecology, organic gardening, prolongation of life, and prevention of disease and aging—does not begin to capture the immediate and galvanizing effect to change one's life for the better. There is no more excuse to grow old, to be ill, or to die long before our time. One of the most important foundation textbooks in the training of I.B.S. Teachers of Biogenic Living.   7.50

All three volumes are available from the International Biogenic Society, mailing address: P.O. Box 849, Nelson, B.C., Canada V1L 6A5. Please add 15% for postage & handling ($1.50 minimum). Checks in U.S. funds only.

APPLICATION FOR ASSOCIATE MEMBERSHIP
INTERNATIONAL BIOGENIC SOCIETY

Please return to: *I.B.S. Internacional*
                     P.O. Box 849, Nelson, B.C.
                     Canada V1L 6A5

*Name*_____

*Address*_____

*City, State/Prov.,Zip/Code*_____

*Age*____*Profession*_____

*Previous Experience*_____

I am interested in:

_____*becoming an Associate Member of the I.B.S.*

_____*becoming a Teacher of Biogenic Living.*

Enclosed is my annual Associate Membership fee of U.S. $20.00. Please mail my membership card, your current issue of the Periodical Review, *The Essene Way,* and my copy of *The Essene Way-Biogenic Living,* my "Guidebook," textbook, and encyclopedia of ancient wisdom and modern practice.* I understand I will receive a 20% discount on all publications as an Associate Member, but only if I order *directly* from I.B.S. Internacional.

Please make your check in U.S. currency out to
I.B.S. INTERNACIONAL.

P.S. The only reason we ask your age, profession and "previous experience" (whatever that means) is just to get to know you a little, as we may never have the chance to meet you personally. If you don't wish to answer, it's OK.

*If you already have *The Essene Way-Biogenic Living,* please choose any other book from our current catalogue for your I.B.S. membership gift.

183

RECOMMENDED BOOKS FOR STUDY

Many members who cannot attend the International Seminars because of distance or limited means are interested in a systematic program of home study. The following books are recommended for such a program, and provide an excellent foundation for study of *The Essene Way of Biogenic Living,* especially when coordinated with the methods outlined in *The Art of Study: the Sorbonne Method.* Also, it is recommended that these books be read and studied before attending the *International Seminars on the Essene Way and Biogenic Living,* held annually in various locations for I.B.S. members, teachers and friends from all over the world.

Please send me the following books:

_____*The Essene Gospel of Peace, Book One* $1.00

_____*The Essene Gospel of Peace, Book Two* $7.50

_____*The Essene Gospel of Peace, Book Three* $7.50

_____*The Essene Gospel of Peace, Book Four* $5.95

_____*The Essene Way-Biogenic Living* $8.80

_____*The Biogenic Revolution* $9.50

_____*The Chemistry of Youth* $7.50

_____*From Enoch to the Dead Sea Scrolls* $5.95

_____*The Essene Book of Creation* $4.50

_____*The Essene Code of Life* $3.50

_____*The Essene Science of Life* $3.50

_____*Essene Communions with the Infinite* $4.50

_____*The Essene Book of Asha* $7.50

_____*Archeosophy, a New Science* $5.95

_____*Books, Our Eternal Companions* $3.50

_____*Cosmos, Man and Society* $6.80

_____*Search for the Ageless, Volume I* $7.80

_____*The Ecological Health Garden, the Book of Survival* $5.95

_____*The Art of Study: the Sorbonne Method* $3.50

_____*Total*

_____*Add 15% for Postage & Handling (min. $1.50)*

_____*Total Amount Enclosed (U.S. Funds Only)*

Please address all orders and correspondence to:

I.B.S. INTERNACIONAL
P.O. Box 849, Nelson, British Columbia, Canada V1L 6A5

*Name*_____

*Address*_____

*City, State/Prov., Zip/Code*_____

All orders must be pre-paid. Minimum order: $5.00, minimum postage and handling: $1.50. Please make check, draft or money order in *U.S. currency, drawn on a U.S. bank,* out to *I.B.S. Internacional.* Allow four weeks for processing. Members of the International Biogenic Society may deduct 20% and *active* Teachers of Biogenic Living may deduct 40% (both must have valid membership cards for the current year). Dealers and distributors, please write to above address for discount information. All sales are considered final.